A Mother's Tears

Living After the Murder of My Son

MARYA FREDETTE

The image represents me: A CRYING MOM. The tears of blood streaming down my face represents the blood of my son, Michael Carreau who was violently stabbed to death. The roses depict my five remaining children. The Spider webs resemble the two tattoos that Michael had on his elbows. The insects detail those which were found on his decomposed body. I am cradling a skull with eye glasses and intact teeth. This portrays the skull of Michael and the glasses he wore. The teeth were used to forensically identify his body. The large time piece refers to the last time I saw Michael alive, whereas the small clock face represents the estimated time of his death. The cross and Rosary beads reflect my Catholic upbringing. One arm of the cross is shaped into a pointed knife edge, representing the weapon used to kill him. The ribbon reveals the date that Michael's body was found by hunters.

Tellwell Talent
www.tellwell.ca

ISBN
978-0-2288-0785-8 (Hardcover)
978-0-2288-0783-4 (Paperback)
978-0-2288-0786-5 (eBook)

Dedication

This book is lovingly dedicated to my son, Michael Carreau, who was found cruelly murdered on 5 November 2011. To this day, the murderer(s) have not been brought to justice, and his case was declared unsolvable.

To all parents of missing or murdered children who desire closure for their pain and anguish.

To my love, Kelly, who gave me strength, believed in me and supported me through my emotions in pursuing this project.

To my five children, Robert Jr., Jean-Francois, Marie-Josée, Yohann and Kelly-Ann, who gave me support, patience and appreciation.

To my brother Johnny and my mother Carmelle who have been there since the beginning, who surrounded me with their kindness and helped me ease my pain many times through my darkest days, and who encouraged me to continue.

And especially to my parents-in-law Keith and Linda, who reaffirmed the notion of unconditional family love and support.

to

Melinda

Table of Contents

Introduction

Life does not belong to us, just as love and death do not either. To this day, I firmly believe that "To be born is not just to come into this world, but to come into life." How life unfolds is unique to each person, but life has two certainties: a beginning we call birth and an end we call death. What transpires between these two events is up to us as individuals. We can either make the best of it or the worst of it.

I am sure that one of you has been touched by death in one form or another. For most, death normally appears toward the end of their lifetime. For me, I never thought that I would face death so early in my life. Unfortunately, this became an early reality; I had to endure the death of my son, Michael Carreau, who was savagely murdered when he was twenty-two years old.

When a child dies from sickness or trauma, the first thing others do is provide comfort and empathy to the bereaving parents. But when a child is murdered, people become guarded in their support, because conjecture and assumptions can reign freely.

It can be difficult for us (parents) to establish with certainty that our loss has arisen from a criminal act. But, some of us have to live with the additional strain of cruel gossip postulated by the general public which makes our pain more severe. I wish to this day that those individuals who made their opinions out of ignorance could know what we went through as we, during that indeterminable investigation, were filled with shock, anger, and sadness.

A few weeks after my son's atrocious murder, the multitude of terrible opinions that followed started to develop into a fear inside me, a fear that my family and I would be murdered next. This fear began to overtake my being, it began sticking to my skin, impossible to control. Eventually, it felt as though I was not living life but meagrely existing, day to day, moment to moment.

With this book, I want to share with you my inconceivable and lingering journey, my frightening nightmare and the outlandish train ride which surrounded the disappearance and death of Michael. From the minute he went missing to this present day, it has been as tumultuous as a roller coaster with no exit. Seven years of emptiness, personal regrets and hatemongers who plagued my family and me. So many times, I found myself being hurtfully put down by others, leaving me aimlessly wandering through life. It was as if I were standing there without happiness, filled with fear and absolutely no hope. Each day after Michael's disappearance was as bleak as the one before. Many questions remain unanswered to this day. Most painful of all, I remain unable to rid myself of the terrible image of Michael's body lying face-first in a ditch near an abandoned train track.

Surprisingly, through this ordeal I developed an enduring strength I never thought I had. This strength permitted me to hear, see and share the fragmented details surrounding his unnecessary death.

As I write this book, seven years after, justice has not yet been served, the investigators have decided to dismiss his case and, as it is known, designate it as a cold case. My immense desire is that one day his savage killers will be held accountable for their actions. I sincerely hope the law will find a suitable punishment to honour Michael's violent death, while finally allowing me to get off of this train ride; in other words, to find closure. Even if the years ahead are still extremely heavy in my heart, I hope that I will never be inflicted with death again.

Another belief I hold pertains to the birth of a child, where a new story begins. It can be filled with happiness and jubilation, or it can bring turbulence to the lives of the parents. There is no perfect rule book or instruction manual for being a parent. There is also no manuscript or guidelines teaching how to deal with the disappearance and death of your child, regardless of age. It is simply unfair when our beloved children die before their parents—when we see them die at the height of their youth, breathe their last breath with so many things that we haven't imparted to them, pass away with their lives ahead of them leaving their parents grieving. For lack of a better choice of words and in the context of the course of life, it is unnatural for parents to outlive their children.

When death occurs, it does not make a difference whether your child is two or twenty-two. The loss and emotions are the same. We bereaved parents lose a part of ourselves and never fully heal.

While scripting this book, I realized how much strength we need to go through disappearance and death, and how the frightful healing process can be different for everyone. For parents who like me have suffered the loss of their child: I sincerely wish that this book will provide them solace and help them with the course of healing, rebuilding and restoring their hearts.

In addition to my story, I want to delve into the myriad emotions that I experienced during my tortuous journey and show to others that we can move past death, and that things will eventually get better.

I believe that this manuscript can help all parents, even those who have not suffered a loss but who are smart enough to reaffirm their blessing. Life is fragile, enjoy every minute with your children while you are still able.

Finally, I want to provide some form of self-reflection for all grieving parents in this world and get them to question: After death, how would my child like to see me? Because I sincerely believe that if you are happy here, they will also be happy, wherever they are.

Sincerely,
Marya Fredette, 2019

My Childhood and Life with Michael

Chapter 1

I was born in Montreal, Quebec at Hospital Charles Le-Moyne in the Longueil district. I was the middle child of three, the oldest being Johnny and Dayle the youngest. Our family was deeply rooted in Francophone traditions and the Catholic Church. My early education was undertaken at an English Catholic elementary school for children whose parents were in the Canadian Armed Forces. My father was a sergeant in communications at the St. Hubert military base.

At that time, children began formal schooling around the age of four. The education we received in early grade school encompassed all the usual academics but were offered only in English.

One of my most memorable school experiences came during my time in Grade 1 with Mrs. McMullen. I found her name hard to pronounce in English, since up until the start of Grade 1 we predominantly used French at home. It may have been the new experience of being in school with other students for the first time, but the ambiance of her classroom stood out amongst the rest of my time in grade school. After singing the national anthem at morning assembly we would return to her classroom to sing other songs as we sat in a large circle. While singing, we would have to pick a dance partner; I often chose a little blond boy, Mike. I began to develop a crush on him. I would imagine getting married to him one day and living happily ever after, the common conclusion to most fairy tales and stories. I even started to imagine that I would see the outline of his face in my cereal, grilled cheese sandwiches and the bubbles of my late-night hot chocolate.

For the most part, unfortunately, my early childhood was not like others, since it was scarred by my father's alcoholism. My father was a heavy drinker. Along with episodes of verbal and physical abuse, I would often be a witness to acts of domestic violence towards my mother. Many times, during his violent outbursts my mother would draw attention to herself to protect us as we hid under our beds, hearing her scream as he beat her.

One of my father's military co-workers, would often come over to our house to stop my father. This friend knew my father well and knew of his violent tendencies at home and in public bars and restaurants. This individual secretly liked my mother, allowing her to call him if she were in trouble, which usually happened when my father would come home drunk and became enraged.

Often my father would return home in the middle of night, abruptly waking my brother Johnny and me. He would force us to do chores and clean the house. He would demand that my mother make him food, and then he would find some reason to start assaulting her. My mother would always try to conceal her injuries in public and would not confess to the abuse to local authorities. One incident that remains with me to this day was a time when my mother refused to cook for my father after he returned from a night of drinking. As we hid in our rooms, we heard her shouting, "Stop! Stop!" while he beat her, and then we heard her scream. That night, he used brass knuckles to punch her. Our bedroom door was left ajar, and through the crack I could see the blood running down my mother's face. Later on, that night, my father had picked up my baby brother, Dayle, and threw him at the wall to try to stop his crying. Like most of the nights, I would end up urinating in my bed or on the floor out of fear, as I was scared to death of my father.

On that night, my mother had managed to call my father's friend who intervened before the police did. I remember him grabbing my father and throwing him against our living room window. The glass broke and he ended up on the front grass. This was enough to stun my father so he could not continue in his drunken rage.

The police didn't arrest my father as my mother did not want to file a report for domestic violence. But on this occasion, my mother was taken to the hospital to be treated for severe lesions, bruises and physical cuts from the trauma inflicted by the brass knuckles. After this skirmish, my father was taken away by the military, after which we did not see him for seven years. We later found out that he had been transferred to an army base in Vancouver, British Columbia. From what I heard, this was at the time the military's way of protecting their own soldiers from civilian prosecution, and keeping things concealed from the general public.

We did not finish the remaining school year in St. Hubert, we moved to La Beauce, a small township situated about 100 km southeast of Quebec City, where my mother was originally from. My mother was a seamstress, and quickly found good employment that was sufficient enough to provide for the four of us. As my dad rarely paid child support, when my mother received money it was barely enough to buy food for a few days. As the years progressed, my mother re-developed a relationship with her first love, Henry, her high-school sweetheart. They dated for many years until he passed away from leukemia. I was at that time about fourteen years old.

The same year that Henry died, I encountered my father, whom I had not seen for seven years, at the town's community centre where he was playing music for a christening. It was a Sunday afternoon. I was the happiest little girl in the world, but at the same time scared to death to see him. It appeared as though time had healed most of the wounds created by him early in my childhood. I would say that I felt a sense of relief that he was still alive; for a long time, I thought that he may have been dead and our mother had chosen not to tell us. My dad played guitar and sang for a band; at that time, he was playing Western music with the popular band Paul Quirion and His Musicians. When I entered the community centre, I heard the band playing and recognized my father's beautiful voice. As I ventured toward the music in the basement near the recreation area, I saw a glimpse of my father. I walked into the middle of the dancefloor hoping to get a better look. Immediately, our eyes connected. When he saw me, he froze instantly, and was unable to continue with his set. I sincerely didn't know what to do. After a couple of seconds, he was able to continue playing, and quickly resumed his timing with the other musicians. After the set was finished, he came over to me to say hello. I chose to stay and talk to him, although I was guarded and beyond arm's length. We talked for a short time, then I left with my friends to play games at their houses.

I returned home that night and promptly told my mother that I had ran into my father. I became aware that my mother still had feelings for my father. I knew she would want to see him again. A short while afterward, my mother went out to see the band, which was playing at the hotel La Villa du Repos near our house. It was ironic that my father's band was playing there. My mom ended up talking to him and forgiving him, and she began seeing him again.

My mother wanted to heal our family and agreed to rejoin with my father. The first few months were ideal, but my father never stopped drinking, and again he resorted to his habits from the past. My mother, with help from her family, got my father to move out of the house, and again we became a family of four. As time went by, my mother began to think less about my father and eventually started dating a gentleman, Denis, whom she would later marry, and he has remained her husband since. Denis is a quiet, likable man and quickly became our surrogate father as he spent more time with us at our house.

One Sunday afternoon after returning home from a day with my friends, I found my drunken father at our house. He had subdued my mother and Denis with a gun and had tied them to chairs in the living room. He was screaming at them, threatening to kill them both if my mother didn't come back to him. Being older and the only child my father would listen to, I convinced him to put his gun away, reasoning with him that he would spend the remaining years of his life in prison if he followed through with this action. I knew that my father was trying to treat his alcoholism. I went to a couple of Alcoholics Anonymous meetings during his short stay with us, but they were to no avail, and this proved that he had relapsed back to a significant degree. As we resolved the incident and tried to peacefully reason with my dad, I managed to call his parents and his Alcoholics Anonymous godfather. They instructed me to place him in a taxi and send him home, which at the time was the residence of his parents. Completely broke and unable to pay for his own taxi ride, I said to the driver who drove him that his parents would pay the bill upon their arrival. As my father got into the taxi his temperament changed, he was saddened and embarrassed by that afternoon's behavior and he realized that any chance of a relationship with my mother was done. I still remember that afternoon vividly: Just after he got into the taxi, he rolled the window down and, speaking directly to me, he made a promise that he would never drink again. To this day, to his credit, he has held his promise. He has been sober for thirty-eight years.

Two years later, at the age of sixteen, I met Robert, whom I would marry before completing my high school education. As I recall, eight months after meeting Robert at a local bar we moved in together and got married.

Three months later I gave birth to my first son, Robert Jr. I was only seventeen years old. Giving birth to my first baby was a horrible experience. Everybody told me that it wouldn't be painful, and that it would be easy and quick to give birth. I endured so much pain for my first delivery, pushing out an 8.9-pound baby with no epidural, yelling my head off from dreadful pain. The baby was huge, the delivery became distressed and they used forceps to pull him out. I ended up with over forty stiches and was not able to sit for a few weeks.

Amazingly, I had our four children in a span of five years—after Robert Jr. I gave birth to Jean-Francois, Marie-Josée and Michael, becoming a mother of four at twenty-one years old. Rarely home, Robert was a good husband to me, but as time went on, he slowly became distanced from his responsibilities to me and the children. Robert was a truck driver and always on the road. He normally arrived home late Friday night and usually left on Sunday afternoon. We were lucky if he stayed for dinner on those Sundays. Robert was raised by a truck driver as well, and he wanted to follow in his dad's footsteps. So, the day I told him I wanted to go back to school, he strongly protested. In his mind, it was my job to be a full-time mother and his job was to be a full-time trucker. His answer was clear: "It is not blood that I have in my veins but diesel fuel." Months later he got into a truck accident. I was devastated and very scared of him going back to driving. He went several weeks without working and walking. His leg stayed injured for many months because he developed osteomyelitis.

The accident forced him to reorient his career, and he decided to go back to school, as did I. As a young couple, this experience was difficult for us and we slowly began to realize that we didn't know each other. Tasks for the house and the kids were a nightmare. To make this worse, we were fighting over the simplest of things (e.g., how the meals were cooked). Overwhelmed with arguments, I felt sick as though I didn't want to eat anymore. In fact, we were not able to resolve anything during our fights but kept having the same fights over and over again, accomplishing nothing.

We consulted with several therapists, but it didn't work. We were both raised in violent, unloving, dysfunctional families, so it was hard to choose the right path when for all your life you had no example of love, laughter and proper parenting. As time went on, we began to grow apart, each with different perspectives on life and how to raise the children. Eventually we separated, and I assumed the role of single motherhood at twenty-eight years old with four children.

I think we were doomed from the beginning of our marriage, and the endless fights only had the power to make our relationship much worse. We can all transform our relationships for the better, but if they have never existed in a healthy way it is harder to accomplish. If we were all to believe that love is good for our health, I think we would be constantly working towards love with greater dedication.

My life is now filled with love and laughs and real examples of parents that have raised their kids with a devotion to happiness. My in-laws have now been together for fifty years, and it is so adorable to see that he still holds her hand and opens doors for her. You can see and feel a deep love between them and for their two children. Every time they see my cheri (Francophone for "honey"), they submerge him in hugs and kindness, with his dad still calling him "sunshine." They are always in an optimistic mood, know how to cheer you up and always find a positive solution to every problem.

I wish we could have raised our children in the same way, and that every human could have the chance to learn that love and happiness really exists, and that two people can be there for each other throughout life. Looking back, Robert and I were in love but we didn't know how to support each other based on the examples of our parents. Perhaps they never had any either?

Michael was raised in a divorced family and there was a lot of discord that neither his father nor I were able to change. We tried so many times that we came to a point where we had drained our love. I regret all those years that I spent fighting with Robert, and I regret not taking more time for my children.

After divorcing Robert, I began to feel a deep sense of disappointment in my life. I began to think that I had accomplished nothing and had cast my ambitions and dreams aside. It felt as if time had suddenly slapped me in the face, asking, "What have you done all these years?"

When I was younger, I was always good at academics. I found learning easy, thus always obtaining top grades and awards. After spending a few months soul-searching and recalling my love of learning, I decided to take my life back into my own hands again. I decided to return to school, not only to complete my Grade 12; but also, to have a decent education from which to build a meaningful career.

With help from my brothers, I managed to hold down a number of jobs in the hospitality industry, mainly in bars and restaurants. Eventually, as the kids progressed through grade school, I finished my degrees in technical college where I obtained engineering degrees in mechanical conception and structural design. I was thirty-two years old. For a number of years, I held two jobs: mechanical engineer by day and bar owner by night. This took away from my time with the children immensely. But being a bar owner is more than just an occupation, it is akin to a marriage. You have to be there all day, every day. Within a few years I opened up a number of other bars, eventually running them full-time, leaving my mechanical engineering career behind.

I was exceptionally successful as a business owner, quickly growing my business to six bars in two years. My niche was to open bars in manufacturing locations, renovating the interior and exterior, and staffing it with pretty waitresses and bartenders. This turned out to be the perfect recipe for the demographic of that areas.

During this time, I met Frederic, a labourer at the saw mill. He was a regular patron at one of my establishments. Within a few years he and I had two children: Yohann and Kelly-Ann, but unfortunately, I was forced to leave him since he developed a substance abuse problem. I did not want my children to be raised in an environment akin to what I had experienced and witnessed as a child. To this day I still ask myself: Why do some women choose to have spouses that resemble their fathers? Why do we as women love so much that we disregard everything and everyone around us, repeating our bad experiences from the past?

Our Last Memories

Chapter 2

I was 45 when Michael was taken from me. Over the past seven years, his assailants still have not been brought to justice. In the months when I was finishing this book, I received a heartbreaking decision from the police: Michael's case was declared unsolvable. The last hope I had to be able to arrest and convict those who were primary suspects had been dismissed. As it happened, it was too difficult to establish all the circumstances, authenticate the virtually non-existent evidence and corroborate all the results to present them to the legal system. At the time of his disappearance we were faced with the impossibility of finding his body quickly, making it impossible to trace his assailant's DNA on the scene. The forensic autopsy supported the hypothesis of homicide—essentially, they could demonstrate the cause but did not have enough proof to apprehend any suspects. I truly feel that in this world there is no justice for the victims and their families of violent crimes. The coroner's official report stated that Michael died from multiple puncture wounds (stabs) to the thoracic region. I guess the gossip about him being beaten and stabbed to death is true.

A year before he passed away, Michael and I owned a bar in St. Gedeon de Beauce, from December 2009 to August 2010. It was a beautiful little place where people were amongst the kindest people you could ever meet. One of Michael's bucket-list items was to have a bar and follow in my steps. He loved entertaining people, music and making drinks. But after six months, both he and I quickly came to the conclusion that being 21 and a bar owner was not the best combination for a young adult. He wanted to go back to school and began reducing his hours at the bar, so we finally decided to sell it. I think we made the right choice, as bars are not easy to manage and it's practically impossible to not drink with your clients. At that point, I returned to my job as a sales representative and Michael ended up registering for school. I was contemplating an early retirement while Michael was working towards his dream job.

The last week I saw Michael was the week of 12 September 2011. I can remember that Monday like it was yesterday. It was a beautiful autumn day with little morning frosts, which were quickly softened by a generous sun and a blue sky. The colour of the trees was beautiful and temperatures were in the 20s. It was the perfect time to take care of the garden, go for long walks and enjoy the scenery of the spectacular Chaudière River and the magical colour of the trees.

Benefited by personal triumphs and financial independence, I purchased a sports car that my children loved. It was outfitted with ground spoilers, loud exhaust pipes, a custom metallic-gray paint job and a fantastic stereo system. I remember Michael asking me to give him my car as his first, and so would often remind me that he would buy it when it came time for him to drive, although he was not in a hurry as it was too expensive and he wanted to concentrate on his studies. That day, I was driving home from the BMO bank on la 1ere Avenue in St-Georges. I noticed Michael coming out of the Carrefour Jeuness Emploi office, which was right beside the bank. He was full of happiness and in high spirits. He had just learned that he had been accepted for his courses and would be going back to school to pursue his interest in culinary arts. Michael intended to complete his course and then work as a chef on a cruise ship so he could travel around the world and entertain and cook for others. I think that assembling people around a table and cooking food created happiness for him.

I honked to gain his attention, rolled down my window and asked him if he wanted a ride. It was a five-minute drive to his apartment on the Avenue Chaudière, just behind. The view of the river and nature from his apartment was astounding; whatever colour you could imagine from a colour palette of orange was there. The magnificent scenes deserved a round of applause for putting a little warmth into a fall day. He invited me in for a coffee to visit and catch up. We unpacked his groceries in his kitchen, which he kept very clean. I knew his instinct for cleanliness would benefit him in his culinary career. As we talked, Michael revealed that he was planning a Sunday dinner at his apartment for me, my mother and my brother Johnny. Michael was especially close to his uncle. Johnny did not have children for the first seventeen years of his common-law relationship, and he treated Michael like his son.

Michael was not materialistic. He would have given anything to anyone in need. He had a wonderful generosity and an innocence about himself, so it was easy to take advantage of him. Many times, in the bar, I had to remind him that it was his bread and butter and that he shouldn't give out free rounds all the time. But it didn't matter to him as long as the clients were happy.

Throughout Michael's early childhood, Johnny would spend many nights a week at our house, helping prepare dinner, giving the children baths and reading to them before bedtime. Johnny was my saviour; he helped me right after Michael was born, since I was weak from the caesarian section that brought Michael (my fourth child) into this world. Johnny played the role of the children's father since Robert was rarely home.

I left Michael's apartment under a barrage of hugs, telling him how proud I was of him for his decision to return to school and for his acceptance to the culinary program. Michael and I had a good bond. He told me most of his inner secrets. I was fortunate enough to watch him enter into early adulthood. He knew that I was always concerned about where he was going and who he was associating with. He knew that his safety and wellbeing were first and foremost in my mind. For me, his past years were especially happy. I was noticing more and more how he was maturing and how much progress he was making with his life. He was stepping into independence and becoming a wonderful young man.

To this day, I remember some advice I gave him, advice that I still want to state to many young adults: Do not focus on aesthetics, but rather on internal strengths and values. Focusing on good looks is not the only key to success; you can be attractive in the eyes of others if you concentrate on being natural, confident, well-mannered and educated.

Often Michael would remind me how important that was for him. He loved the tips I gave him to optimize his physical health and his abilities. And yet, from time to time, I would have to reassure him: "You're a beautiful kid, Michael." He had a hard time with his self-esteem, and we had to work hard to help him. I think we don't practice that phrase enough, in the house or when they leave the nest. This holds especially now—youth are so influenced by social media and instant gratification.

I still remember a glimpse of his smile, pure and kind. I left him, anticipating our dinner on Sunday. Michael was planning on making us a meal consisting of parmesan chicken, bruschetta and chocolate brownies. Nobody made bruschetta the way Michael did. It was simply delicious.

The night of Thursday, September 15, Michael called my house and asked for me. I was out riding my bicycle, making the most of the exceptional weather. Yohann answered his call and they spoke briefly before Michael requested to speak to Kelly-Ann. She was sleeping in her bedroom, and Yohann chose to let her sleep. Michael really liked his younger sister; he used to call her his "Mini Kelly." He then asked Yohann to tell me that he loved me and all of them. I still wonder to that day what he wanted to say to me. Yohann remembers that phone call like it was yesterday. To this day, Yohann still carries a sense of guilt that haunts him, and he thinks that he should have asked him what was wrong, as he felt that something was bothering him. He said he was calling from a public phone at the shopping mall on 1st Avenue.

Later that night, I was out with a group of friends celebrating the birthday of my friend Sauveur, who was also a bar owner. Along the way we visited another bar, Bar 4000, finally ending up at Bar Le Merlin. Shortly after arriving, I noticed Michael was there by himself playing on the slot machines. I went up to him and greeted him with a hug. As we talked for a short time, I noticed that he seemed a little pre-occupied with something, but he didn't want to tell me what was going on. So, I sadly returned to my friends for the night's festivities. Shortly afterwards, Michael came and told me that he was leaving to meet someone at another bar. In the little city of St. Georges, bars are all gathered on the same street.

He seemed in a hurry to meet this unknown person. He gave me a quick hug, said goodbye and left promptly. This would be the last time that I saw him alive. He was murdered on that night a couple of hours after I saw him.

The following Sunday, my brother and I drove to Michael's apartment. Shortly thereafter, my mother and her husband arrived. To our dismay, Michael was not there. We thought it was strange that Michael would be absent when he had invited us to dinner. As we were standing in front of his apartment, one of Michael's female friends, Emilie, a tenant in another building, caught us in the parking lot to inform us that she had not seen

Michael for a couple of days. Emilie used to spend almost every night with Michael, hanging out and chatting about their days. We decided to go to my mother's house for dinner, where we were met by my step-sister, Sabrina, who informed us that Michael had failed to show up for work at her farm for his Saturday and Sunday work shifts. This was very unusual behavior for Michael. During dinner, we collectively came to the supposition that Michael may had decided to go on a last-minute road trip with friends or a girl, but I felt weird, as it was not his habit to do this and his culinary courses were starting soon.

While enquiring about Michael's strange disappearance and gathering information of where, when, who, etc., I heard through one of his friends, Ray, that he had started dating an older woman. Actually, she was the mother of my younger children's friend. Some say that there are many reasons why younger guys fall for older women. The first, plausibly, is that they miss their mother. I knew that Michael was heartbroken when I began working in Toronto and he chose to temporarily stay with his father.

Another reason for choosing mature women is to avoid drama. So, I was not surprised at the many times he mentioned to me that he preferred older women. Back then when I let Michael advocate for himself, his viewpoints were very precise and right to the point. He was not necessarily looking for a younger or older woman; his preference was not for a certain age, but rather for a "no strings attached" friend. Apparently, he just thought that in his situation this was the perfect one for him. In my opinion, age has nothing to do with relationships. I remember him saying that he had found that special someone. She was so beautiful, with a wonderful sense of humour, and she was, to him, very sexy. She was giving him the space to talk about anything, which was very refreshing and engaging for him. On another occasion he mentioned, "You do not know that you can be attracted to an older woman until it hits you."

Sometimes you do not even realize the disparity in age until a couple of weeks or months later. He knew she was older, but I think the fact that she was there to offer affection, devotion and intimacy was a blessing. She showed him how to take better care of himself and was a good reflection on him, a major key to building confidence and self-esteem in a man.

At the time, I was myself in a relationship with a younger man, with an age difference of eleven years. I had no idea that I could be attracted to a younger man until it hit me. He certainly didn't have to work hard to convince me.

Michael liked being stimulated by her sharp intellect. They enjoyed going out together, having a level of conversation where they could both be themselves and laugh for hours. He also mentioned how he loved that she knew herself and thought she had so much more to offer than a younger woman, and that she was looking for different things. He liked the fact that she was playful and not looking for a provider or a father for her kids. My son's confidence and attitude definitely helped give him an upper hand in that area. He was very direct, clear and focused on what the principles of life were. And I am sure if I asked him again, he would say the same thing.

If you ask any man what a mature woman has to offer, he would certainly say emotional stability, the ability to see things, and their level of honesty in being true to themselves. My handsome partner, who is also a couple of years younger than me, revealed that his enormous love and respect for me comes from all the things I made him realize. He says that he is now more grounded and realistic and that I made him understand how important it is to make someone else happy and feel loved for who they are, and how mutual self-love is contagious.

He now recognizes how stressful and ridiculous it was trying to have meaningful conversation with younger women. His brief experimentation with younger females was fraught with endless head games and immature behaviour which turned him off. I think men like the fact that we invoke a kind of emotional maturation and a depth in things which some spend a long time searching for. The fact that we are more experienced with life, know exactly what we want and say exactly what we think is a must for a younger man, or a man of any age. We know what we feel and why we feel it. The important thing is to wake up every morning and think that you have the world on a string. We have nothing to prove to people. Life can end anytime, and my story is proof of that.

Since Michael's murder, and when I began writing this book, I asked him on so many occasions: "Who ended your life? Maybe her, maybe you…"

I am sure that someone knows something. If only they could have the courage to talk. If only they were able to feel our pain. Grieving the death of a child is a significant life event; however, not everybody has experienced that form of grief. To understand the loss and grief for a young adult, your child, who has been missing and whose murderers were not found, is in my opinion far worse. We parents go through so many things during the progression of a police investigation and the legal process. Sometimes we are unable to find quick and appropriate support. We are unable to find understanding and awareness in the community or the media. But the most devastating thing is not even being treated like a victim and having no compensation for our needs. Finally, we the families of missing and murdered children just want time to relieve our sadness and for our loved ones not to be forgotten. In my opinion, the system is made to protect the guilty, not the innocent. And, unfortunately, nobody has a scale big enough to measure our pain.

His Sudden Disappearance

Chapter 3

Through the course of the next two weeks, I returned to my normal schedule with work and my two younger children. I made repeated attempts to contact Michael on his cell phone, but the only thing that I would reach was his voicemail. I remained in contact with Johnny, my mother and many of his friends who had similar luck to trying to reach him.

As these weeks progressed, I mastered, perceived and comprehended that something terrible had happened to him. I am unable to explain how I came to have this feeling, possibly it was maternal instinct or my special bond with him. During this time, others around me made an effort to reassure me that he was going to return, but deep down I understood that something was not right and that he would not return.

On Saturday, October 1, I received a phone call from my mother around noon to inform me that she had received a telephone call from Michael's landlord, Yves, enquiring as to Michael's whereabouts, since he had failed to submit his last two rent checks, required bi-monthly.

Yves informed my mother that the outside of Michael's door was covered with private notes from friends enquiring about where he was, and for him to contact them. Upon hearing this from my mother, my body tensed and I developed goosebumps over my arms and legs. My instinct told me that something bad had happened to him. Michael was responsible and would not bypass two rent payments, nor go on a road trip for such a lengthy period of time without informing me of his itinerary.

In a broken voice, I managed to say, "Mama, Michael is dead."

My mother was upset by my statement. "You cannot say that, he is not dead, he is probably on a trip with his friends."

"No, Mama, he is dead," I solemnly replied as I began to cry. "I am going to go to the police to sign a declaration for a missing person."

After hanging up the phone, I called my brother Johnny. "I feel that Michael is not going to come back, that something tragic has happened to him."

Johnny replied, "I have the same impression too, this is not like Michael."

He briefly paused, and then with deep sadness added, "I didn't tell you because Michael made me promise not to tell you because you would get worried." I listened intently. "The Wednesday before I last saw him, the day I bought my new motorcycle, Michael was with me and we grabbed dinner at my place. He was very worried that someone was after him and asked me about taking one of my handguns."

"He what?" I asked in disbelief.

Johnny replied, "Yes, he asked me for a gun, but I refused because he wouldn't give me an answer as to why he needed one." I continued to listen.

"Besides, my guns are registered with the province and I didn't want to get involved with anything that would hurt my credibility," Johnny stated firmly.

I started weeping as we talked for a few more minutes. After I ended my call with Johnny, I called the municipal police to declare that Michael was missing

Constable Giguere informed me that it would be better if I went to the police station after dinner, since that was a very quiet time and they would have an abundance of time to receive me and take my information. Later that evening, after I had made arrangements for my children, I went to the police station where I was met by Constable Giguere. To this day, I wish adult disappearances could be treated the same way as they are for a child. Sadly, it does not work that way. The fact that Michael was an adult made me face a lot of obstacles. The first thing they said, and it made me think, was that he may have needed the freedom to rebuild his life without informing me. In addition, they told me that they generally considered that an adult has the resources to protect himself and is less vulnerable than a child. They explained that the situation cannot require the same priority or urgency for the police. We sat for an hour as he took notes of Michael's description and what had transpired over the past weeks. Along with Michael's description and contact information, Constable Giguere asked me if Michael was suicidal, suffering from depression or wanted to harm himself. These questions are part of the identification process. Unbeknownst to me, a belief held by police at that time was that suicide and depression were often closely related to the disappearance of individuals.

Regardless of their age, the protocol for filing a missing person's report is the same: stripping the person of their humanity so they simply become numbers on identification sheets. Data collection is relatively straight-forward: physical description, clothing worn and last known whereabouts. However, after the process things diverge drastically; disappearances are handled differently according to the age of the person in question. For a young child it is fast, as an Amber Alert is issued immediately; however, for an adult it can take days. In my son's case, it took five days for his report to be publicized. In my opinion, those five days could have been critical to finding him alive. The municipal police didn't take his disappearance seriously enough and they speculated that he was away on road trip, while deep in my heart I felt that he was not with us anymore. He was now gone, and I could feel my heart breaking. I couldn't go on when I would think how his life was taken. At night I would pray for his embrace or even just to see him again. But every time I would close my eyes, I could see his gentle smile the day I left his apartment. He might have been out of sight but he was always on my mind. But the police chose to ignore my fears and concerns. And to this day, I still despise those officers for their ignorance, as my son was already dead.

After police took down his information, they began formulating hypotheses regarding his whereabouts. One such hypothesis was abduction. Police will often enquire if the parents have significant wealth and assets that could be used for ransom purposes. In my case, and upon revealing my financial position, that hypothesis was quickly dismissed. While I had a decent amount of money, I wasn't rich. Another hypothesis that police often query is that the missing person had committed suicide in an isolated location. Again, I expressed my view of Michael's personality and zest for life, explaining that any third party who knew him would be hard-pressed to believe that Michael would commit such a selfish act. And yet, for many of the following days the media—specifically the newspapers—used suicide as a primary theory, as it would boost their sales. The media went so far as to research my family's history, depicting a false image of abundant dysfunction between all our members. One thing is certain: The general public is naive. This is a value judgement, but rumours and gossip spread very quickly amongst the citizens of the area as soon as the media began releasing their falsehoods. I resent the media for their poor taste, misleading comments and unprofessionalism during these difficult days. I do not know if I will ever forgive them. The final hypothesis that was raised by the police was murder. For me this was daunting, but I felt that it was the truth.

Constable Giguere finished our meeting by informing me that he was going to forward his report to the appropriate department of the municipal police. Days later, I was contacted by a Constable Lacroix of the missing-persons department. During these few days, my mental status was coloured with a mixture of sadness, despair and terror.

Early the following day, I received a telephone call from the landlord, who was pressuring us to empty Michael's apartment as soon as possible because he wanted to rent it out to other people. I contacted my mother and Johnny to make arrangements to collect Michael's belongings and clean his apartment.

It is crazy what you have to do when your grown child disappears. You are lost and imprisoned by your own thoughts and have no idea where to start. In your acquired state of shock and disarray you have to make the most of your time—researching for facts between circles of friends, family and coworkers. You desperately attempt to generate new leads or information that can be used to help in the investigation.

I was trying to spend time confirming Michael's last days, but I was not permitted to have information from his employer because he was an adult. I even created many scenarios of fake calls pretending to be a fellow employee, but due to privacy policies of the company I was unable to get any pertinent information. I found myself at an impasse, completely messed up and in a dead end. I was so frustrated and helpless.

If we can get more information doing our own investigation into the disappearance, should we be able to locate friends, relatives and loose associates? Certainly, contact them immediately, pretending to be an old friend, first love or family member enquiring about their last location. If I can give you advice: Please write everything down. Start your search with their immediate friends in the city. If your search does not produce any interesting paths, go with your feelings and gut instincts. Because even if you contact the town hall to check the population list, it is not less one person that is going to make the difference, even if you have to go out of your way. Again, prepare a small call scenario to make your contacts sensitive to your request. But people are so dumb in those situations.

In the days after Michael's disappearance, I began following his history by looking through his Facebook account. As we exhausted all avenues of searching, I began to realize that there were no answers, he was just not there anymore.

In hindsight, placing an immediate call to the provincial police or a private search agency would have proven easier and simpler—they have a well-honed process and they will know how to create leads and follow tracks that the stupid municipal police have missed. They would have been much more efficient at finding my missing son. But again, in my situation this was hard to do since in their arrogance they wanted exclusivity in Michael's case. What an abomination…

It was now thirty days after his disappearance. The sky was as blue as a lagoon; the wind was feeling nice and warm over my skin. For the beginning of October, it was a fantastic day. My day started with a nice breakfast on a patio, which you rarely see in Quebec at that time of year. I was haunted by the feeling that I would never see Michael again. It was one of the worst feelings ever.

I was trying to focus on my itinerary for work but completely ended on the opposite side. I stopped to have a coffee at a restaurant around 10 A.M. and all the regular patrons were there talking about his disappearance. They were saying that it was drug-related and that he was a drug dealer who owed money. I was sitting there literally wanting to rip their heads off one by one. Those people had no clue who I was and who he was, but they were judging Michael based on what the newspapers and social media were saying. Astonishingly, there was even a person who started talking about revenge by the Hell's Angels. Not only was I torn by the judgement they were directing toward my brother, but I was also drawn to the evidence that could make this a possibility (as I will delve into in a later chapter).

My heart was convinced that I would never see him again, but I also had to deal with the fact that my brother, whom I had cherished all my life; the person who helped me so many times with my poverty; the one who provided me with food when my fridge was empty; the one who was Michael's best uncle who spoiled him so much every time he saw him; the one who Michael admired all the time; the one who gathered all the family together, making us laugh and enjoy the amazing moments; the one who would give even his shirt to make us feel better; my hero who saved me from Hell was maybe the one who had sent my child to his death. In my head I was a turmoil of emotions.

When you go through the disappearance of a child you feel as though you have no help. To make matters worse, there can be others who ignorantly judge you, worsening your pain and loneliness. We simply have no idea who to turn to and no place to be listened to. When Michael went missing, I had to deal with journalists who wanted to concoct a story so they could become the most-sold newspaper in *la Belle Province*. We fight against time, inconsistency and opinionated people who have no clue what we are feeling. It's like driving your car with no destination in mind. More often than not, I would yell out Michael's name in my sleep, eventually waking up in a cold sweat, alone in my thoughts.

So, on that day, overwhelmed with emptiness, I left the restaurant with so much pain and anger. I tried to hit on a couple of businesses to do my sales pitch to try and get a paycheque to provide for my two children. I just couldn't bear to go back home, so I finally ended up at my mother's house at 3:00 P.M. I drove so fast to get there; thank God there were no children playing on that gravel road that day.

When I arrived, I stopped my car, and at the same time I stopped breathing. I was in so much pain. My legs were so weak and my heart was pounding so fast. I climbed the six stairs, banging my shins on every one, opened the front door and started yelling and crying, with nothing but a memory of him and a dream. My mother was shocked. She asked me if I had found him or if the police did, but I couldn't answer. She kept asking, "What's wrong? What happened?" But there I was, down on my knees and telling her that I would never see him again. There's wasn't much more that I could say, I realized that I was there without Michael. "I cannot face another day, Mama. All I want is to find him. Can you feel the love but also the storm in my head? I am losing my mind, all I want is to find him, his body, so maybe we can turn back and say goodbye."

I was sure that the unimaginable had happened to Michael. My body was aching all over—my legs, my ribs, my back, my neck. I then finally said to my mom that somebody had killed him. I felt it over every inch of my body. I was in so much pain. I had never gone more than two days without knowing where he was. He would do the craziest things on the planet but he always called me for help, advice or love. He even called me on the day he got kicked out of his first apartment, laughing about it, but I was so mad. I said, "Michael, that's not funny, you're young and you need to be responsible and pay for your stuff." Then he promised that it would never happen again, that he would pay his due from now on. "And if you are short on money, just ask."

His answer was, "Mom, you do so much for me, I can't ask you that." At that time, he had a lot of anger towards his dad. He hated his father for all the pain he had left him from the lack of support in his life. I explained that this was his life now and that no one was responsible for his actions. I thought it was a great idea going back to school, and that he would have made a superb chef. When I got back to reality, I explained to my mother the dream that I was constantly having, and I talked to her about the last text Michael had sent me. My dream started with Michael running through the forest. He was running and screaming, trying to run from three guys. One had a long pony tail like Bernard, the one who bought our bar. Then Michael tripped face-forward in the mud.

In my dream I was never able to see the guys. But I knew that dream was the truth. It looked so real and it was making my body ache. Then I started to ask myself, "If you died running away from them, then how long had you been there? How long had you suffered in that pond? How bad was the pain?" My mother was trying to convince me to stay positive and to not think that way. She said that I shouldn't even think about that and still have hope. That day, erroneously, I asked my mother to leave me alone. Everybody was after a story, a picture or an event to give them hope that Michael was still alive. I just didn't feel it. I asked her to do the tarot. Ironically, for my first card that day, the card representing the present, meaning what is going to happen, I drew the four of diamonds. Michael's Surname is Carreau, the French word for diamond, and he was my fourth child. But when my mother told me the significance of the card, there was not even a hope left. My mother and I start crying and she understood. When you draw the four of diamonds it means you are going to attend the funeral of a close person. My only wish was to find Michael's body and have closure.

I had to go through so much misery because of the media and my ex-husband Robert's family. They had never been present in Michael's life. They always assumed that he was a lost cause because he smoked weed. In order to boost their reputation, Robert's family began talking to journalists. I was completely against having Michael's photo given to the media, but his defiant cousin decided to pass it on to them. That day I was with my two children, trying to make the most of our day by focusing on positive thoughts. We were having a good day and barely talked or heard about Michael. We could park in our driveway without being hounded by journalists, which was rare. So, we decided to sit in the living room and watch the news. We were sitting and laughing and chatting when suddenly our hearts stopped. Michael's picture was right there on that television, that box, that thing. They were saying that they were looking for him, and if viewers had any news, they should contact the provincial police or them. I was shocked, so were Yohann and Kelly-Ann. We started yelling and crying; we couldn't believe that someone who had nothing to do with Michael all his life had the audacity to do that. I wanted to rip their heads off their shoulders. People just don't understand how much pain and anger this can cause.

I realized again in that moment that some people have no feelings for the close family of people who disappear. They just want to be famous. They just want to be heroes in the eyes of others. I was so mad. I had the gut feeling that Michael had died, but somebody had the nerve to publish

Michael's picture without my permission. Our night was filled with tears and rage against those individuals. We were so hurt, but that was just the beginning of the nightmare. The morning after, Michael's younger brother had a hockey game at the little arena where we lived in St-Côme-Linière. Arriving at the arena, I noticed that everybody was looking at me. Soon, they started asking if it was my son who was on the posters that had been posted throughout the building. "Do you think he is dead? Do you think he was into drugs?" Question after question, it just didn't stop. My head started spinning as I tried avoiding them to shield Yohann and Kelly-Ann. I lost it. I started ripping down all the posters that were in the arena. I started calling them jerks and cruel. My friend had to shake me to get me back to reality. I was hurt and had so much hate for those people.

I wish at that time I knew the magical phrase that one of the investigators taught me: How would Michael like you to be? How would he like his mom to shine? That was one of the most powerful sentences *I have ever heard.*

Almost every day now, I refresh my memory with that phrase and it enlightens my day, even on very dark ones. When you miserably glance at the television news and you hear about the trial of a guy in Florida who killed 29 innocent students in high school, you think to yourself that it would have been nice if you could be there and say that magical phrase to all those parents. I guess the key to becoming stronger is to learn daily and handle that impossible pain. Try, and I really say try, to direct our energy in a different direction if we don't want to sink into anger and bitterness.

So, like Mark Manson says in his book *The Subtle Art of not Giving A F*ck,* HarperOne, 2016, in life we have a certain number of fucks to give so we must choose them wisely. We must grab pain by the shoulders and look into what's left. We must live with entertaining horror stories, profanity and ruthless humour about incompetents.

Venturing into his Apartment

Chapter 4

Later that week, my mother, Johnny and I met at Michael's apartment, which had sat dormant for almost a week. Constable Lacroix and Yves the landlord met us there to lightly inspect the apartment. Again, it was one of those beautiful warm sunny days, hotter than normal for that time of year in La Beauce. As we approached his front door, we couldn't help but notice all the notes on it. Written on various pieces of paper with different colors of ink, in styles of writing that were both arguably male and female, were notes from the full complement of Michael's large circle of friends. The landlord opened the door for us and left immediately, letting us do our thing. As we entered Michael's apartment, the first thing that grabbed our attention was the stench of rotten food and an almost musty smell that resembled an expired cat box. At the time, I did not realize that the smell we were encountering was plausibly that of a decaying body.

As we ventured further, we could see that Michael's apartment was in shambles, a far departure from his immaculate housekeeping and hygiene that we as a group were accustomed to seeing. Immediately, my mother uttered, "Something bad happened here." I felt the same. Something crucial had happened to my son. It felt like he had been murdered or subdued in the apartment.

With each step I took, I became more aware that I was literally speechless; I thought I was losing my voice. It was as if someone was watching me. I knew something bad had happened. I could feel it; I could sense it.

My mother came to my side and made a remark about how things were misplaced in the apartment. My mother had a lot of intuition which often allowed her to feel and predict things. Most of the time her intuition was right. I tried desperately to find his beautiful burgundy duvet covers and the bedding I had given him, but they were missing from his king-sized bed. His small closet was empty and most of his clothes were lying on the floor or in a black garbage bag. The bedroom stank; it was almost impossible to tolerate that disgusting odour. It was the type of odour that forces you to pinch your nose, a smell that even bleach cannot wash clean. This remarkably widespread stench was disturbing my mother. Like a mantra, she began repeating, "It smells so bad in here; something bad has happened here." I trusted her instincts better than my own. I knew her feelings and words were right.

As we started to scout around Michael's tiny apartment, we noticed that a half-cooked steak was left in a frying pan on the white stove of his little kitchen. When I saw this, I said, "This is not Michael's habits; he would not waste food like this." In the fridge there was moldy cheese, rotting perishable food and a milk carton that was well past its expiry date. On the little kitchen counter, the fruit bowl held half a dozen blackened bananas, expired as well. Turning our attention to the infinitesimally small kitchen table, we noticed two half-finished Budweiser beer bottles and an ashtray with cigarette butts. Again, we knew this was out of the ordinary, since Michael did not smoke cigarettes. It doesn't take a creative intelligence to know unequivocally that somebody else had been there.

Beside his brown couch, which had been mysteriously pushed and angled away from the main wall, we noticed a white shoebox with a pair of brown hiking shoes. The shoes had a thick buildup of mud on their soles. We knew these were not Michael's, as he had huge size-fourteen feet. These shoes were a size seven or eight. Draped over the back of one of the dining chairs was a black leather vest, an article of clothing we had never seen before. Michael did not wear leather clothing, nor did he wear vests. The long curtains in his living room were drawn closed, as if to prevent people from seeing inside the apartment. On the patterned floor of the living room were red stains which we thought were from spilled fruit juice or cream soda pop. It was later confirmed that it was not blood, but arguably evidence that some form of physical struggle had happened in the living room.

My brother Johnny was in disbelief, like me. Immediately, he called Yves to enquire about the missing computer and television. "Where is Michael's laptop and 52-inch flat screen?" In an unpleasant tone, Yves answered, "I only took the TV, I wanted to make sure the rent gets paid. I will give it back to you when I get my rent!" Unhappily, Johnny asked, "What did you say to my sister? Are you without pity? You have upset her." It is so unfair to be attacked in such circumstances, when we are the perfect target for bullies. Yves replied, "I told her to clean up the apartment and I want my money right away!" I was imploring God for us not to clean it, I knew that would wash away any remaining proof that might help us find the killers.

I pleaded with Constable Lacroix to take notes, keep evidence, take pictures, but he simply ignored me and left us to our own actions. Lacroix' reply to my request was met with a sarcastic rebuttal: "No, I don't think so, he is probably off on a road trip somewhere, or growing some pot in a friend's basement." I was numb with horror. Rookie officers could have done better. Why are some people so immovable with their beliefs? I wish I could have taken a video of our conversation. Possibly I could have shown it to his supervisor at a later date to show how unprofessionally this case was handled. Police are supposed to serve the public. Instead, he did nothing, and everything we were telling him was blindly disregarded.

The feeling that was growing in my heart was that something terrible had happened to him; frankly, I knew that he was already dead. I was unable to control my emotions. I fell to my knees and began to cry hysterically. My brother Johnny knelt beside me holding me in his arms. Unable to think clearly, in a state of shock and confusion, we left the apartment soon after.

There were enough signs to reveal that at least one person if not more had been in Michael's apartment, presumably on the night of his disappearance, or maybe after assaulting him and commandeering his apartment door key.

Even for the average layperson, one would be suspicious upon seeing that his bedding was removed and nowhere to be found. I sincerely believe that it had been used to conceal him as he was transported somewhere. Why didn't the police take any of this seriously? Who would steal blankets from a bed? To this day, I have my suspicions. I also believe the landlord may have taken them before we arrived. The blankets could have had bloodstains, and he did not want to have any problems with the police, or leave him unable to find a new tenant for the apartment. I would surmise that, with all that evidence in the apartment, if Michael's case had been handled correctly his killer or killers would be in prison now. Impartial or too selfish to do the right thing, the municipal police officer was very incompetent, unprofessional and simply ignorant. I know that those responsible for Michael's death would have been found if the municipal police of St. George de Beauce had believed me and not dismissed the overwhelming physical evidence in his apartment.

When I look back, I think about that landlord, his hopelessly dogmatic statements about Michael and his declaration of securing Michael's flat-screen television for the purpose of collecting owed rent. Why could he not have settled on the basis that my son was dead? I have no respect for him whatsoever. He was an unforgiving jerk, a masochist, a control freak only interested in his own financial gain.

Michael's apartment sat for another week before I could return and begin cleaning. I could not figure out a way to avoid this. In hindsight, I should have listened to my own instincts and never allowed any of us to empty the apartment, anything that had to do with touching, contaminating or removing his belongings. Today, those responsible would be served by justice. Why are we blindfolded by fear and misconceptions of death? I had no power, no witnesses and nobody that would have seen this crime. I wish at that time I could have had quick and appropriate support and the investigation would have started then and that legal procedures would have been followed. But they were refused to us.

As we were finishing packing, the landlord came and returned Michael's television in exchange, of course, for the rent owed. This individual has never understood the real nature of my conflict. We drove Michael's belongings over to my house and placed them in my basement of my beautiful home in St-Côme, listening to silence while hardly speaking to each other about what we had seen and experienced at Michael's apartment. Other family members and friends were still convinced that Michael was alive, and a tiny part of me still held to that belief as well.

In the days that followed, my continued loss of appetite became worse as my emotions began to fluctuate, arising from what I had witnessed in Michael's apartment and from the gossiping of the general public. I was lost and again left hopeless.

Our Futile Search

Chapter 5

The following Wednesday after my first visit to the apartment, was like any other workday for me. I was woken by my alarm clock at 6 A.M. to my favorite local radio station, Cool FM. I took a long hot shower; my body was sour and was aching everywhere. I tried to eat a healthy breakfast, prepared my usual lunch—granola bar and fruit—and jumped in the car heading for work. As I was driving, the latest newscast came across the airwaves. It had its normal rendering of national and provincial news. During the show, I recalled that the province of Quebec had lowered their delinquency age to twelve years, since most youth crimes at that time were committed by adolescents of that age. The last headline I heard surprised me: It was the municipal police's missing persons alert for Michael. Likewise, during the morning the police published a report on their website, on social media and in the newspapers. In their articles and posts, the police had said that Michael was suicidal. It was particularly disturbing, as Michael was anything but this—he was the complete, polar opposite.

The Alert was as follows:

> At the request of the family, the Saint-Georges police department is looking for 22-year-old Michael Carreau, who has not been seen since September 8th. He left his home in Saint-Georges, leaving everything behind him and his relatives have been without news since.
>
> According to his mother, he may have suicidal thoughts and discouragement. He is single and does not have a driver's license or a vehicle.
>
> Physical description: Caucasian, brown hair and brown eyes, measuring 1.88m and weighing 80kg. Always wearing jeans, a T-shirt and dark sneakers.

It was a very basic description of him. Information that should have been mentioned was that Michael wore glasses and had two tattoos on his elbows of spider webs. As you can see, this case was taken very lightly by the municipal police.

Later on, that morning, when I was on a staircase at a client's building, I came across one of my former co-workers who began revealing his outrage. That weekend, his niece had been hit by a drunk driver and she was in a coma in hospital. He had no idea if she would be able to survive.

Feeling his sadness, I started to hyperventilate, and had to run outside for fresh air. As I sat outside my throat became increasingly knotted. I found it hard to swallow, and my heart started beating louder and louder. I came to the realization that the world is full of violence, accidents, sickness and death. I knew that my co-worker may never see his beloved niece again. My feelings of loss resurfaced immediately. Deep inside me, I felt that my son would never come back again.

That feeling is hard to explain, especially to someone who has never experienced loss. This emotion is triggered quickly by related events, and it consumes your thoughts and your body constantly. You become a zombie trapped in your own thoughts. I felt like the lead singer of the Cranberries when she sings, "In your head / In your head / Zombie, zombie, zombie…"

In fact, during those times such emotions are actually part of your survival instincts. In a positive sense, emotions can be used to inform us of dangers or to appropriately choose the right response to a threatening situation.

That day, I went to the police station for an explanation and to express my disappointment with their public awareness campaign and their lack of communication. After arriving at the police station, I again felt ignored by Constable Lacroix. I then became frustrated and started pushing chairs over. Within minutes I became very vocal, demanding to see the chief of police, since Constable Lacroix was still disbelieving everything I had disclosed, and disregarding my belief that Michael was murdered somewhere.

I demanded a reason for the choice of words that were used in Michael's missing person's description. I thought that a missing person is when the whereabouts of a person are unknown, and for whom there is a concern about their safety, their life or their well-being. But as it turned out, the municipal police did not subscribe to this definition. This stemmed either from a lack of training or their preconceived opinions regarding Michael's lifestyle and acquaintances.

Eventually, Chief Tardif revealed to me that this was the way they did things. He said, "If people are aware that he may be suicidal, people are more likely to help him if they come across him. I guess it's like a marketing trick, to get the public's attention and to publish more things." I had no choice but to accept this explanation and go along with their process. But there was an abundance of evidence telling us that he didn't do this; Michael's departure was not voluntary and therefore I was constrained by the fact that he was now an adult and not under my wings anymore.

In the days that followed, our family and friends organized two searches, called *battues* in the Francophone community. *Des battues* are systematic searches, conducted in groups, of the area surrounding the missing person. In Michael's case the first was in Parc des Sept Chutes, in St. Georges West. Michael loved this majestic park, spending much of his free time walking and riding the trails with his bicycle. The second was around his apartment on Avenue la Chaudière, in St. Georges East.

During the *battues*, we wanted the municipal police to participate but they declined, still believing that this was not a real missing person's case. My son Jean-Francois joined us during these searches, giving us tips on how to conduct them. He had acquired these skills through his experience as a combat soldier following two tours in Afghanistan with the Canadian infantry. As we concluded the final search, I realized that my greatest fear was becoming increasingly valid: Michael was gone. I just wanted to find him so badly! I wanted to feel him, and to find his body.

On Halloween day I was returning from a nice walk that I was hoping would help me with my anguish. Walking in the forest has many benefits for me. I hold that nature walks are good for your physical and mental well-being. If you have the chance one day, it's worth it to go with your friends and family to see *La Belle Province*, that is, Quebec, with its little villages filled with amazing restaurants, markets and cultural activities. I suppose that to a small degree the forest helped alleviate my sadness for a short time that day. As I walked steadily along the roadside, a car pulled up alongside me. It was Constable Morin of the Sûreté Du Quebec, of the provincial police. I had known him for a number of years. He had heard about Michael's disappearance by word of mouth and enquired as to how I was managing. After a long conversation, he suggested to have Michael's case transferred to the Sûreté du Quebec, since they had better resources to investigate missing persons. I of course agreed, wanting to find out the truth as soon as possible. So, the day after, 1 November, I went to their office and was received in a very professional manner. I was immediately welcomed by the *tactics team,* where a number of the agents had worked with my brother Dayle in prison a few years prior. It was finally reassuring to know that somebody would take me seriously. I met different constables and was interviewed several times. I knew they had the same feeling as me and knew that Michael was dead. The only thing we had to do now was find his body and his assassins.

Some of Michael's friends also started to line up at the Sûreté du Quebec to provide information, revealing their worry and consternation. That week, I visited the police office almost every day on my way back home from work. To this day I have no words to say how grateful I am to the members of the Sûreté du Quebec and Constable Morin. Compared to the municipal police, their diligence with me and with Michael's case was unprecedented. One of the agents is now a lieutenant and he is the most understanding police officer I have ever met. Back then he always had the right words to cheer me up, and the right phrases to tell me that Michael was still there.

Soon after taking on the case, Lieutenant Jean Couture authorized a search of Michael's apartment with their entire forensic team. As it so happened, the apartment was still vacant; Yves had failed to find new tenants. During the inspection, they dusted for fingerprints, took photographs and used ultraviolet light illumination to search for blood and other body fluids. They asked for the black leather vest, but I'm not sure if they took the muddy running shoes which we had left in the apartment after we had removed Michael's items. With all of these techniques and the physical evidence, they were unable to make any conclusions as to what had really happened in the apartment. Everything was gone and contaminated with other fingerprints. The whole crime scene had been handled wrong. Handled like beginners. They iterated to me several times that they wished they could have started the investigation. All the inspectors that worked on Michael's case are still convinced that there was enough evidence in the apartment necessary to find the killers. And we shouldn't have been forced to clean it by the landlord or the incompetent municipal police of St-Georges.

At that time, I started reviewing the obituaries in the newspaper. I was hoping this would give me some guidance on how to compose Michael's obituary when the time came. Or perhaps in the headlines there would be an unidentified body found somewhere. Ghoulishly, I read about the passing of other people, reaffirming that I was not alone. Moreover, there were other people out there experiencing the loss of a family member. Eventually I stopped this undertaking, since it did nothing to ease the sorrow that was starting to invade me.

During those days the only pleasure I could anticipate was his Facebook account, where I was looking for evidence of his disappearance or for his friends to talk to. Maybe I was also looking for a post from him. I remember one day seeing Michael online. I began freaking out. I immediately asked a couple of his friends online if they were seeing him as well. And they confirmed they were seeing him too. It was so weird, and so scary.

Eventually, I came to the conclusion that it was the murderers. They were using his laptop and had managed to access his Facebook account. Maybe they were tormenting us or maybe they were stalking us? The day after I went to the provincial police to inform them of our finding. Within hours, someone logged out of Michael's Facebook account, which would never be reactivated again.

While this was happening, I started to develop a sense of guilt, which cursed every fibre of my body. I thought so many times that I had failed in my most basic duty: I had not been able to be there for that call or answer that text. I wish I could have known that Michael was in an unsafe situation. And on that particular night of 15 September 2011, I wasn't there to protect my son.

I was living alone with the ultimate tragedy, trying to cope with the usual symptoms and stages of grief while there were so many issues surrounding his disappearance. The thought of murder made my parental bereavement particularly difficult to resolve. But at least this time I had the provincial police listening to me and trying to find some answers. There had never been one time that Constables Couture, Morin and their team didn't return my call or didn't receive me. They were, like me, dedicated to finding the truth.

Disappearance of a child is gut-wrenching! It can be exacerbated and complicated by feelings of injustice, the understandable feeling that this loss never should have happened. Shortly after a child goes missing, most parents experience excruciating pain alternating with numbness, a dichotomy that may persist for months or longer. Many parents who have lost their son or daughter report they feel that they can only "exist." They simply "go through the motions." Functioning day to day seems nearly impossible. It has been said that coping with the death and loss of a child takes the largest emotional toll on a person, more so than death of a parent or friend.

The relationship between parents and their children is the strongest bond that humans hold in life. Much of parenting centres on providing and caring for our children, even after they have grown and left home. A child's death robs you of the ability to carry out your parenting role as you have imagined it, as it is "supposed" to be. You may feel an overwhelming sense of failure for no longer being able to care for and protect your child, duties that you expected yourself to fulfill for many years. When I returned to work after a couple of days, it was with the slow, painful walk of a cripple. My words came with difficulty, each sale I presented was a hurdle which I struggled through. I was lost and couldn't concentrate. It seemed as if everybody else knew something or had heard the truth about what was going on. Their young adults were flourishing, working and studying, and they were all there securing their future. In comparison to mine, everybody else's life just seemed so perfect.

There were also those who looked at me with large, tender eyes, people whose gaze I avoided and with whom I didn't want to talk about my missing child, as I was scared to be judged, so I would walk stiff-faced out of their businesses, garages and stores. I was shy about saying what I was feeling. Back at my house, I would spend most of my time staring dully out of the window in my living room. At other times I would simply stare at the ceiling of my bedroom, my back resolute against sympathy aimed in my direction, with absolutely no hope.

Quickly my sorrow started to transform into anger. I wanted people to stay away from me. I resented their kindness, their determined advances into my space, anything they said that expressed solidarity, the slightest reference to what had happened. I wished I would have had nothing to do with social media, the newspapers and the uninformed opinions of others. People are so judgmental and never go with the facts. They are easily influenced by conjecture and assumptions without knowing the truth. The hardest inference I had to deal with, due to the municipal police bulletin, was that Michael was suicidal and that he probably took his own life in a secluded area. Another problem was from the gossiping of people who believed this was related to my snitching brother (which I will reveal in a later chapter), and the notion that Michael's murderers would resurface one day to kill my entire family.

From time to time, I recall the ongoing visits I had from my friends and family trying to reassure me that he would return. How useless those were to me at the time! Little did they know it did not help me one bit. I remember one of my friends telling me she saw him walking on the street downtown. She persisted, saying that he was alive, and she ignored my instinct that he was dead. Simply useless, I felt devastated, isolated and misunderstood and wondered how different it would have been for even strangers to be better in their reassurances, rather than standing there in my face and gossiping about my son all the time, as their negative, fictitious and narcissistic opinions meant nothing to me. I cannot accurately remember anyone who came to see me. Although all their gestures were grandly appreciated, I could not connect with them on the same level. The companionship I sought was that of fellow sufferers. I wanted to talk to people who, like me, had experienced that kind of feeling, who had a missing or dead child, but at that time I did not know anyone like me. Once again, I was alone with my terror and discomfort.

I was feeling like a mama bird nesting an incubated egg. My egg had hatched somewhere, and I was completely vulnerable. Somebody somehow had taken my egg and I had no idea where it had gone. One after the other they were leaving my house. But I was there in the pitch black, frightened by the death of my son, every night, wide awake, I could hear the owls and all the other nocturnal predators. It was like sleep and food were not sufficient, they had become scarce. You don't want to suffer, but at the other end I was risking my own starvation. But with that wait, you just skip days and starve.

On the other hand, I wish we could be like nidifugous birds. When their babies hatch and are sufficiently advanced, life permits them to leave the nest a few hours after, or at the latest a few days after. But for us, mothers of human babies, it is different: They never leave the nest. They say that a human writes their testament of happiness on the very first day of their birth. I never took time to write mine, neither did Michael. Even now, I do not think I can describe the endless nights before 6 November, peppered by multiple visits to the investigators, shaped by my silent home and all the hours that I spent looking for him, the collective silence with my brother Johnny, his brothers, his sisters and my friends. People would all gather around my dining table or the living room couch. I have no clear memory of those days. I just remember having weak legs some days because I would walk for hours, looking for him or to release my pain and anger. I remember my hands being numb, my head going empty and a frantic burning itch unfurling beneath my skin. Then, for hours, no sound, no warmth and no painkillers—nothing made any difference. My brain was completely shut down; I thought that I would never regain function. A hazy disbelief shrouded everything; my mind was doing its best to cope with the outside world as if I could bear no more data entry in my system. I just wanted to find Michael and his body and, once and for all, turn the page and forget about what people were saying.

Over the next few weeks I was numb. My emotions were fluctuating uncontrollably. I would experience outbursts of aggression followed by episodes of sadness and despair. I cannot begin to explain the hours that I spent weeping and crying myself to sleep. Thankfully, with the assistance of my family and my children, people had limited exposure to my tears. I started to develop a hope that he had not suffered too long, that possibly his death was quick and painless.

Since the first day the landlord called, I was convinced that Michael would never come back. Having that call that said Michael had been missing for two weeks made my spine freeze from top to bottom. I couldn't stop thinking that he was dead somewhere.

In an effort to reach out for help, I decided to call his father, Robert, to tell him that I was worried about our son. Everybody was talking about it but no one wanted to admit it. I thought that for once in my life, Michael's father would be there to support me, but I was wrong.

At that time, Michael's father was in Calgary, where he had joined Michael's older sister and was living with her. Not the opposite, like the newspapers said. Michael's sister was already there with her husband and their two daughters. Michael's father, along with his wife, had been living with Michael's sister for several months.

The day I called him for his support, I really wanted to hit him with a baseball bat. When I announced to him that Michael had been missing for a couple of weeks and that he should come and search for his son, he refused. He said that Michael must be somewhere growing pot and left the apartment with no notice. He said Michael was a druggie. He never liked the fact that Michael smoked weed and was very judgmental about it.

Every morning when I awoke, I would check my cell phone for texts or voicemails hoping that I could hear his voice again or see a missed call with his phone number. But all I found was nothingness.

With each passing day, I was quickly reminded that he was gone. I found myself falling into a depression as my feelings of guilt worsened. I would constantly ask myself: "What if I had spent more time with him, would none of this have happened? If I had gone to the other bar with him on that Thursday night, would things be different? Would he still be here? Where did I fail as a parent?"

I can still hear his voice on the day I left his apartment after driving him home: "*Je t'aime, Mama. À bientôt, j'espère.*" "Love you, Mom. Hope to see you soon." What a beautiful last phrase, and yet how painful.

Once again, I thought I was losing my mind, that feeling was coming back. It was like someone was watching me and I knew something bad had happened. I could feel it, I could sense it. Michael's death had rendered me speechless. It was not as if I could not find the right words to say, I had no words to say; I knew he was gone. For the most part, I knew there was nothing I could do to bring him back.

But on other days, a sense of denial would overcome me—denial that he was dead, a mere glimpse of hope that what others were saying was true. In all honesty, looking back I found this period of indecision the most troubling of all, since intense emotional mood swings would accompany these alternating mindsets.

Shortly thereafter, I somehow made the decision that it was necessary to avoid other's opinions like the plague. Especially those who thought they knew a lot about Michael's case, and those who thought they knew all about the pain I was suffering. I surmised that, for my own mental wellbeing, it was imperative to listen to absolutely nobody. I had lost trust and faith; I did not know how to speak about Michael's disappearance. Should I use a saddened voice? Or should I use an angry voice? I just didn't know anymore which one to use. By choosing only weak words to give a singularity to this death, and sweetness to the love that a mother has for her child.

The night of Saturday, 5 November, I met some of my girlfriends and former employees. I was invited to go out to help ease my emotions and, for lack of better words, to try to get my mind off of my son's disappearance and probable death. It was the first time I was going back to a bar since I saw Michael at Le Merlin on the night he disappeared. I must say it helped, but only to a small degree. Nonetheless, I am grateful to have those friends still; they are friends for life. I remember that night being particularly nice even though the weather was overcast.

Fall 2011 was so warm in Quebec. We had record temperature highs that year. September and October are my favorite months of the year, especially in my own town, where you can see the beautiful colours of the maple trees. It's a must-see. Quebec City is beautiful all year round, especially in the fall; it has the most spectacular scenes. Shades of gold, orange and red that monopolize the forests, the paths and the fields. The maple, beech and oak leaves explode into colours. Gentle breezes blow along your face and numerous lakes sparkle in the sunshine. One of the best ways to experience the autumn is to cycle, walk or slowly ride your motorcycle along the endless stretches of open highways.

That night, I was extremely vulnerable. I felt as though there was a big threat above my family's head. Two months prior to Michaels disappearance, my brother Dayle had snitched against the most powerful motorcycle group: The Hell's Angels. People were going crazy with their opinions, saying that Michael's disappearance was related to his troubling confessions. I didn't know who to believe. Was it related?

I knew in my head that many other former members had snitched against the Hell's Angles without repercussions. Also, it was widely known that Hell's Angels do not kill the families of snitchers. But there I was with my broken heart laying down on my crumpled bed completely naked and inert, and my useless trembling body was trying to cope with reality while staring dully at the white ceiling.

The Shocking Confirmation

Chapter 6

The day after, Sunday, 6 November, I was awoken around 7:30 A.M. by the sound of my front doorbell. I assumed it was the Jehovah's Witnesses; they would sometimes come to my house to read the Bible. On some occasions I would find this a relief and it made them happy. I was in my bed, my place of solace. My bedroom brought me so much tranquility and peace. It was spacious, with nice wooden floors, teak furniture and Scandinavian décor. As I sat up, my heart began to race. I could feel my heart thumping in my chest. It was an uneasy feeling. I peered out my bedroom window, noticing that it looked cold and blustery. I could hear the wind through my windows and hear the rustling of leaves on the ground. I looked towards the sky, shielding my eyes from the light. Then I observed a car in my driveway.

My driveway formed a beautiful path that was surrounded by big tall spruce trees. In the winter it looked so magnificent with all the ice on them, like a fairy tale. I loved my house. It was built on an acreage. I would often see whitetail deer in my backyard, rummaging and searching for food on the lawn. My house was spacious, my kitchen had a nice patio door and white cabinets. A marvelous stone gas fireplace divided my kitchen from the living room, where I had a solarium with an exquisite bamboo floor. My bathroom had two sinks, and a splendid Jacuzzi surrounded by windows and a skylight. Around the Jacuzzi were tiled stairs with internal lighting to complement the tranquil flavour of the room.

I got out of bed, dressing in a white towel housecoat. Looking through the window, I saw a woman holding a black suitcase. My children were lying down in the living room in sleeping bags in front of the fireplace, which was one of their favorite things to do. My first instinct was that she was an official, someone in power or related to the law. Negative thoughts of fear began to race through my mind—maybe she was here to arrest me? Maybe I had driven my car home under the influence of alcohol the night before? With trepidation, I opened the door and quickly glanced at her from head to toe.

She was dressed in a long black trench coat and had fabulous long black hair and stunning green eyes. She was quite beautiful, with an aura of calmness about her. But her face was telling that there was something wrong. Since she was not accompanied by another person, I knew she was not a Jehovah's Witness. Besides, I wasn't in the mood to be lectured in theology and salvation. But in seeing her standing there, my body became cold and inert. My spine practically froze as if a direct electrical current was flowing through it. I knew she was not here to read the Bible but was here to reveal the truth about Michael. Indeed, she was the bearer of bad news. She was the agent from Sûreté du Quebec who had to deliver terrible news to families regarding their loved ones. I later came to respect this woman highly, since she had suffered an immeasurable loss two years after the death of my son. Her five-year-old daughter died from complications of a tonsillectomy. She stands as a symbol of courage for me, but with her loss and my loss of Michael, I began to wonder again: Where is justice? Where is peace in all of this?

She introduced herself as Constable Theriault, an investigator with the Sûreté du Quebec. She opened her dialogue with a simple question: "Are you the mother of Michael Carreau?" My upper body became immobile, my legs started shaking and my heart stopped for a moment, then began to beat very hard. I could hear the loud noise of my stomach. I could tell that she was here to tell me the news that I had been anticipating for the past two months. I simply replied, "Yes."

After a pause, she invited herself in. She asked, "Is it okay to sit down while we speak?" I nodded in reply. She mentioned that they had found a body and it was of the same age and structure as Michael's description. "I have pictures to show you." She entered the house. We sat ourselves at my beautiful kitchen table, and she began to explain that there was a possibility that it was Michael. As I shall argue, the universe with its "superintendent" had found my son.

Constable Theriault revealed that two hunters had found a body in the local area. The magisterium had suddenly happened. She described the body: "A Caucasian male, early twenties, they couldn't see any distinguishing marks, scars or tattoos, as the body was found in an advance stage of decomposition and it was not possible to determine any physical traits." Her words sounded horrific, but they forced me to ask her aloud the ultimate question: "Is it him, Constable?"

We all presume that after a sudden death it is important for living relatives to see the body of the deceased. But Constable Theriault's stance with these matters differed. She went onto explain to me that based upon her experiences with cases such as these, and the severity of this crime, my mental health could be permanently damaged if I had direct physical contact with him. Therefore, only identification with photographs would be permitted. There were two possible candidates, the other one was a male, who had already been missing for ten years and examination of the body was telling them that it couldn't be him.

Such question is beyond our strength. It is an ignominiously weak point, but to the bereaved, us, the relatives, we find ourselves viewing the body in photographs—but how can this give closure and affirmation of the deceased? Instinctively, I knew from that moment, with her preliminary description of the body and its condition, that if it were to be Michael, I would never touch him again. Even if I knew he died a good person, it was distressing not to be able to see his deceased body in person. I wanted to make sure he was going to paradise to enjoy the supreme virtue of God.

I explained to her, "I need to know the truth, and to see Michael one last time." She reaffirmed that there would be no personal viewing of the body, only pictures. She once again reiterated that to identify him without causing serious psychological shock, only pictures of his personal belongings recovered at the scene would be shared.

Constable Theriault realized that Kelly-Ann and Yohann were present. She suggested that they be allowed to see some of the photographs for identification. In my numbed state of mind, I agreed to let them see the photographs. In hindsight, I should have asked them to go back to the living room, leaving Constable Theriault and me to ourselves, as the pictures may have been disturbing, besides the fact that underage persons are not viable witnesses for identification purposes. She first showed us partial views of the clothing found on the body. She asked us if we recognized any of the clothing. We confirmed that we did. Then, from her briefcase, she took out a plastic bag with two items inside. One was a pair of eyeglasses. When she put the glasses on the table, I knew it was him. Michael's eyeglasses had a little tape from where the kids and I had repaired them a couple of weeks before and nobody could have had the same. She also brought out a leather belt. In an instant I froze, recognizing Micky's stuff. Confirming that he was indeed gone, I stared nervously at the items for a moment, and then uttered, "Those are Michael's." She took them out and placed them slowly in front of me on my beautiful glass table. I still remember the stench of the items. As it turns out this was the smell of putrefied human flesh in the advanced stages of decomposition.

Constable Theriault then took out more photographs that depicted a body on top of grass and dirt. The photographs revealed a body with limbs bent in unnatural positions, obviously indicating multiple broken bones. The skin of the body looked abraded and showed signs of what I would later learn as decomposition. The body was still dressed in jeans, surrounded with the same belt that was on the table in front of us, a T-shirt that looked covered in blood stains, and underwear that was exposed by being pulled higher than the waist. Michael was one of those who wore, as a generational fashion trend, their pants halfway down their buttocks, revealing their underwear. I recognized the underwear with Bart Simpson on them. They were Michael's favourite set of underwear, purchased for him by Sara, his ex-girlfriend. Oddly enough, the photographs had been edited so as not to show the head of the body. I inquired, "Why can't I see his face?" She replied, "If I show you that photograph, it will haunt your dreams for the rest of your life." She refused to show me the photograph of the face, since it was severely distorted from physical injuries and was in an advance stage of decomposition, which I would not have been able to recognize anyways.

Since Michael's death, and relating back to the issue of viewing the body of the deceased family member, I have often come across columns and editorials that discuss this. Many of these writings are opinions, and, although open to debate, I hold the opinion that it should be permitted. When they announce the death of your child it is surreal, it is like a dream. It's the worst thing you can possibly imagine. You can never be completely prepared for something of this nature. But by not having a physical vision of the body, neither touching nor feeling it, it makes it a little harder to fathom.

When death occurs, after a chronic illness or drowning or a motor vehicle accident for example, loved ones may have the opportunity to see the deceased body soon afterwards. In fact, it could be argued that physical contact with the body may help with closure as an affirmation of the death. In many instances people may exhibit a need to lay down beside them, hug them, kiss them, and even try to comfort them. For these people, they do not want the deceased to be alone; they want them to be with someone who loves them. They often feel as though their presence will even heal or bring them back. This is why I think first responders sometimes have to struggle with family members, restraining them from seeing the body. I still wonder what my reaction would have been if I had been at the location of his discovery. I certainly would have liked to have seen his body, possibly to fill in some of the blanks. I have no idea if this is common to all the mothers, but that would be my preference.

For this reason, I asked Constable Theriault before she left if I could see Michael's body one last time. She responded, "No, Ms. Fredette, his body is too far gone." I really believe this would have helped me to a greater extent on that day. Would it have brought me peace sooner? I guess I will never really know. I am still haunted by not seeing him or touching him one last time. As I sat there, I knew that I would have to endure another process: the autopsy and forensic dental examination.

In July 2007, I remember I went to the hospital with my mother to identify my sister's boyfriend, Jean-Francois. My sister, Danielle, had discovered the body of her boyfriend after he had committed suicide. Our job was to provide positive confirmation that the body belonged to him and support my sister. She was in too much shock to provide an accurate confirmation. When we arrived, we were directed to the mortuary, where nurses and attendants were waiting for us. From there, we were led into a small intimate room, accompanied by the coroner, Mr. Garneau, who is now a judge.

The cause of death was suicide by strangulation. It was not easy viewing his body; he had a big noticeable circle around his neck but his body had not changed. His face was discoloured but it was easy to recognize him. When we said yes, it was him, they asked us to leave and that was it. To this day, Danielle says that she has closure, since she had the opportunity to physically touch him when she found him. I never had that opportunity.

Constable Theriault consoled us for a short period before leaving with the items and photographs. During her process, I called my brother Johnny. He arrived at the same moment Constable Theriault was leaving. They talked for a brief moment outside. I have no idea what they discussed but my brother came back inside, hysterical. I immediately called the rest of my family and friends to come over to my house right away. I remember my feet being heavy, my head feeling empty and a frenzied scorching beneath my skin. For hours, I wasn't able to comprehend anything; nothing made anything different.

As I relayed to my family the events of the investigator's visit, I confirmed with them that Michael had been killed. This cemented the conclusion to all of them that he was not returning, even though some of them up to that moment thought he was away on a road trip. Many broke down in tears and the others remained silent, each with their individual emotions and grieving to wrestle with.

Even now I find it hard to completely describe the endless night of 6 November, and the silence that surrounded the table that day as everyone stayed at our house to console each other. There was also a hockey game that day for my son Yohann—that year I was the manager of his team. I called my friend Manon, a mother of one of the team's players, to explain that I would be absent as they had found my son dead. That was the only game I missed the entire season. Yohann, who was an important player and part of the team preferred to play that day. I still can see his face and the determination he had to go play and score some points for his brother Michael. Earlier, the coach had caught word of Michael's death and somehow understood Yohann's need. Coach Dupuis was an excellent coach. That year we only lost one game, and on that day, he allowed Yohann to play as much as he wanted during the game. Yohann scored four goals and three assists. The whole team wanted to win for Michael, and he was well served: They won 25–0. Thereafter, I remember all the parents of the team being very supportive of us, providing me with help, rides and affection. It was a good year in that regard.

I was the victim of an unnatural occurrence: outliving my child. I felt as though a part of me had died. As far as I was concerned, all children should outlive their parents. When parents experience the loss of a child at the height of their youth and beauty, it is simply unfair. Children should be those who grieve for their parents, not the other way around.

In the days following Constable Theriault's visit, more and more information came to light regarding the discovery of Michael's body. I remember going to the obituary page of the local newspaper to examine the only item that interested me: the death of Michael. I devoured confirmation that I was not alone with the death of a family member. Although this did nothing to ease my sorrow, I persisted in searching for answers and listening to the public, to friends and to police for any small piece of information they could release to me. Frankly, searching like this made me feel sick, or psychopathic.

Gossiping in the Media

Chapter 7

Shortly after finding Michael, the media regressed to an all-time low. They contacted an old aunt of mine. She was seventy-one years old. It was well known to our close-knit family that Aunt Marie-Ange had been clinically diagnosed with Alzheimer's disease. The media took it upon themselves to conduct an interview with her when she was clearly not of sound mind to provide any useful information about our family. After the interview the media released a malicious article regarding Michael and our family.

When the children were younger, Aunt Marie-Ange had been a very good person in our lives. During the summer months, she would travel the province with the Beauce Carnival, bringing back dozens of gifts to spoil my children with. In her off-season (late fall, winter, early spring) Aunt Marie-Ange dedicated herself full-time to all four children; they loved her dearly. She was unable to give birth for reasons that are still unknown, thus treating my children as her own. She was a devoted, reassuring and optimistic woman who instilled good values in my children. She guided them along the straight path. She can be proud of that. She was a humble woman with a big heart, and with a dark humour all her own. In life she was simple, without complexities or drama. Her favourite pastime was spending a lot of time in the woodlands where she couldn't resist a wood stove to cook us all good food.

As a grand-aunt, she would always exercise her role as a spare mom and would always help me when I had to work three jobs to make ends meet. She exhibited bravery that was an inspiration to those around her.

I have always held the opinion that the things we read in the newspaper or online can act as a trigger, creating a whole host of emotional responses. For me personally, these things trigger an irritation deep inside me that I cannot really explain. The only thing I know is that suddenly, after that article, it was as if the whole world had gone a little petty, and I felt like the only reasonable people to trust were my family and close friends. I felt so much bitterness, so much aggravation, so much outrage. I really thought that the world had suddenly gone crazy!

Through the years, Marie-Ange had been very good to Michael but became more distant as her Alzheimer's disease progressed. But the media took her comments at face value, while so many other truths remained hidden. She mentioned that she thought Michael had bad friends that were turning him into a drug addict, so his death was drug-related. Another preposterous comment was that one time I had locked the kids out of the house as a means of discipline. These were misleading of course, since Michael's friends were good people. Further, with the locked-door incident, the children had returned to a locked house one day in a rainstorm from spending the entire day in school. I was actually inside, but fast asleep in my bedroom, the side-effect of working multiple jobs. Consequently, they walked in pouring rain to her house for shelter, only a few short blocks away. These comments were twisted into lies that painted a bad picture of me. The truth was retracted by the media a couple of days later, but only in a small article buried deep inside one of their subsequent newspapers.

To this day it is difficult for me to harbour any ill feelings towards Aunt Marie-Ange; she was a great part of our lives and could not be held accountable for her statements during the interview. She passed away, one and a half years later of her Alzheimer's disease

Magnitude of My Brother Snitching Against the Hell's Angels

Chapter 8

My brother Dayle was arrested in 2009, along with 155 other members and prospects of the Hell's Angels in Operation Sharqc. It was an extensive police operation conducted principally in Quebec, and was so named because it bore close resemblance to the counter-terrorism investigation of the same name in 1946. In response to the King David Hotel bombing, British Mandatory Palestine conducted a series of house-to-house searches, intending to deprive the Igrun organization of manpower, hideouts and weaponry. Operation Sharqc was the culmination of three years of surveillance and informant testimony, which allowed these 156 to be brought to justice, making it the largest police operation to be conducted against organized crime in Canada. Police agencies worked collaboratively with the Sûreté du Quebec and the Royal Canadian Mounted Police through the entirety of the investigation. Collectively, it took the efforts of 350 investigators and 1200 police officers working over three years. As an aside, five of those investigators have worked on Michael's murder case and with my brother Dayle in prison.

My brother's involvement with the Hell's Angels started in 1984, one year after I got married. He was only fourteen years old. Like me, his childhood had been severely scathed by our father's alcoholism and ensuing domestic violence toward our family, especially my mother. During his first year, he would frequent the club as a hang-around, aspiring to become a Hell's Angels member. He longed to be part of a family, which up until then he had never experienced. In his teens, he spent most of his time at the local clubhouses to develop close ties to its members, providing him with masculine examples to look up to. Notwithstanding, my brother was also an avid fan of powerful motorcycles.

During the early years of his involvement, Dayle would never share any details regarding his location or activities. It was intriguing seeing him so drawn to the club and their lifestyle. I often asked him questions, but his strict code of silence made it impossible for him to reveal any information. I recall one time I asked him, "What do you like about it?" He simply answered along the lines of, "Our group is like a big gang of brothers; we do things that bring me adrenaline," and then he would lower his head and wouldn't divulge any further information.

As an outsider looking inward at Dayle's affiliation, I was able to make drastic observations, seeing him closely involved with this organization and stepping into it as a member. Additionally, he was successful in progressing through the junior ranks and was not intimidated easily by the police. As he would say: "You need to love heat!" simply because the police were always trying to pick on them or make them divulge information about the club's activities. Further, he told me he had taken the oath of secrecy regarding the club's members and he was going to be a big businessman and do a lot of deals. This oath remains in my mind; we frequently tried to convince him to quit, but he would blindly ignore us. He desperately wanted to become a member, even if later he decided to disassociate himself from this organization. He was pledged to keep secrecy. During this indoctrination process he was directed to read pamphlets from the world headquarters of the Hell's Angels. He said, "You read it and then they take it away as soon as you are done." I was also informed that Hell's Angels also own all property imprinted with its syndicated death-head logo. They have stringent policies regarding usage and infringement of their logo and dress code. For example, members wear black leather vests but they do not own them. The Hell's Angels own the vests. If you leave the Hell's Angels, you must return anything that says "Hell's Angels" on it. I remember that during Operation Sharqc we had to either return everything that belonged to them or destroy those articles with fire, as we were forced to help my sister-in-law recover from the destruction the police did to their house after a search-and-seizure.

In addition to black leather vests, members have to abide by a strict dress code: black jeans, black shirts, black socks and shoes, but no shorts. The cycle of the patches can be very long or short depending on how things go for those members. To finally be accepted into the Hell's Angels, you have to start by being an "official friend," go to their weekly "church" meetings at the clubhouse, exclusively associate with the members (camaraderie), and successfully complete all tasks and challenges that are presented to you. My brother got the whole arsenal, and even a few extras. Through the remainder of his youth and into early adulthood, Dayle became increasingly involved with the Hell's Angels. He progressed through the ranks: hang-around, prospect, striker and then, finally, onto a full-fledged patch (member) in 1998. He became a member of the Filthy Few, or an enforcer for the club. Filthy Few members are recognized as being willing to commit a murder on behalf of the club.

Over the years, I met some of Dayle's Hell's Angels brothers. Contrary to common belief, the Hell's Angels are incredibly disciplined. They go to the gym, eat well and are far from the image portrayed in movies. Their parties are clean, nobody does cocaine in front of you. Most of them are sober; they are just like us. They have dedicated people everywhere and make sure that everything is handled professionally. Their business is selling cocaine, controlling the market, and not losing it.

My brother had several chances to get out of the Hell's Angels. I thought the fact that he became a father would deter him, but after the birth of his daughter in 1999 he was involved more than ever. I didn't know what he was involved with, but I saw him change drastically. He was often away from home on "club business." During his excursions, he would leave his wife and daughter with my mother. He had that unspoken "don't ask, don't tell, don't see" rule. In a very short time, he started having bodyguards and prospects with him when he visited my mother's house. I didn't want to know what he was up to, but I knew that he had more stuff on his vest and his responsibilities had taken over his well-being.

My brother was a Robin Hood to all the members of our family. What he was taking from the life of crime he was giving back to us, the poor and less fortunate. Every time he came to my house or my mother's, he would bring food and order a spectacular dinner for all of us. He loved doing this; it brought him so much joy. He was such an endearing person. He would spread laughter, love and happiness amongst all those around him. He would bring me treats and say, "Here you go, my sister, please spoil yourself and your little ones."

The day I left Toronto because the father of my two younger children was constantly harassing me, Dayle immediately found me a new place to live. That day I left, I opened my fridge door thinking that I only had one litre of milk and a loaf of bread to survive on. It was a day I will always remember; I fell to my knees and prayed for a miracle to happen for me and my children. I was devasted.

I left Toronto in January; it was -32º Celsius. I drove for eight hours straight with my two kids in the car and just enough money for gasoline. I arrived at his apartment where he had filled bags with food and toiletries, and there was a tiny white paper envelope filled with a little extra spending money. My brother spent the greater part of the evening boosting my spirits. I always knew he had my back. The only promise he wanted me to make was to not go back to my crappy relationship, whose substance abuse was at an all-time high. My brother hated people who consumed cocaine, especially those who exposed their family to the behavioural changes and financial hardships that accompanies their addiction. He always encouraged us not to touch it and didn't want any of the children being close to the Hell's Angels, as he was starting to regret his choice to become a member. But for him, it was too late to back off.

Ultimately, Dayle was my brother. He was a big part of our lives and almost like a father or godfather to all of my six children, and they loved him very much. He provided so many things for them, contributing and enriching their lives. I know that I was naive and blind to his activities, but I loved him whatever happened. So that is all that mattered to me at that time.

In July 2011, while in prison, Dayle decided to become an informant (snitch), against the Hell's Angels organization. This was around the time of Michael's murder, and with the speculation of a revenge killing for Dayle's confession many people were—and are still—scared to discuss details about my son's murder and disappearance. People think it will bring repercussions by the Hell's Angels.

Personally, I do not agree with this hypothesis. If the Hell's Angels started killing the nephews, sisters or brothers of the families, it would never end.

The Hell's Angels are a specialized club and do not touch the families for revenge. If they do, it is because they are involved in something that is affiliated with them or owe big amounts of money. They are not the way people think. They do not kill for small amounts of money or kill old people. They kill for large sums of money; they respect the normal citizen. They have better things to do with their time than go after a couple of dollars, which could put them at risk of going to prison. They focus their efforts on their larger business undertakings. That's why they wear patches and crests; so, people know who they are and who they work for and have no guilt about been seen with them. Those patches and crests are hard to earn and they are very proud of them. As a normal citizen, it is best to ignore them. If you do not bother them, they will not bother you.

After my brother snitched, I didn't answer my phone for days. I was so tired of my brother's lies; I was worn out from hearing his story. And by this time, after the murder of my son, my anxiety had gotten really bad. To this day, no one knows why Michael was killed—not the police, not the Hell's Angels, and neither do I. There were, and still are, so many unanswered questions: Did the Hell's Angels tell my brother Dayle that it was revenge? Only the individuals that were with Michael that night would know what happened, and will they talk? "Who will take care of the guy that killed him? Were we supposed to get rid of him, like, kill him?" Who knows? Still unanswered questions, even after seven years.

One thing both the police and I know is that an altercation took place in Michael's apartment. Items that were out of place included cigarette butts, Budweiser beer bottles and a plain black leather vest with no crest or group identity, and they are unable to determine whom the latter belonged to.

The investigators of Sûreté du Quebec and the Royal Canadian Mounted Police are 100% positive that the murder of my son was not related to the Hell's Angels. So, through their efforts, I have come to accept this and stopped questioning my perceived sense of danger.

My brother Dayle was sentenced to twenty-five years in prison. His real heartbreak is that he is not be able to see his children grow up. His children and family life meant everything to him.

After a couple of months in prison, he started calling everybody regularly. He wanted us to drive his kids to see him and for me to take care of them, which became a very scary and difficult task for us. Being driven in a blinded panel van and housed in a secluded building for 48 hours just for visitation was insane.

As time went by, his wife became increasingly distant and perceived him as self-destructive. She no longer had any money for grocery shopping or supporting the kids adequately. After thirty months in prison, around September 2011, Dayle turned in his vest, meaning that he ended his affiliation with the Hell's Angels. For members of the Hell's Angels, turning in one's vest is considered to be a form of treason. Individuals can end their affiliation, but they have to maintain their sworn oath of secrecy. Any violation of secrecy is punishable by death. Of significance, Dayle's action to turn in his vest was figurative rather than literal, in the sense that he had become a snitch to the Sûreté du Quebec.

Prior to this event, Dayle told us on many occasions of his plans to do this. His wife and our family pleaded with him to end his affiliation in the literal sense. We believed that becoming a snitch would put us all at risk. We continued to tell him that he could simply retire and keep quiet. But at the end of the day, he disregarded our advice and did it anyway.

To this day, I resent Dayle to a certain degree, because his actions created a fear in all of us that plausibly wasn't necessary in the first place. It's like saying you should destroy their altars, break your image and cut down your grove.

I am not sure what Dayle's motivation was to become a snitch. Was it to clear his conscience? Or get even with some members he did not like? I thought his decision showed a weakness in his character. He began claiming that he did not commit the crimes for which he was accused. Rather, he told the police that other members of the Hell's Angels had committed those crimes. Not taking responsibility for your actions is not a way to get out of guilt. I did not agree with him becoming a snitch, since the media blew it all out of proportion and possibly could have placed our family in danger. He was aware of the latter, but nonetheless did it anyways. Whatever he told the police, truth or lies, I really do not know what to believe. I think that Dayle probably told the lies as a means of saving face in our eyes and protecting himself, but this only worsened his situation, as lying to fix his previous lies only revealed more about his crimes and opened up further avenues of investigation for the police. To our family, it was as if he was trying to deny who he was. It would have been easier if he had kept his mouth shut, paid his time in prison and retired from the group.

As the weeks went by, Dayle began to reveal to the Sûreté du Quebec names of individuals involved in organized crime in Montreal and various other cities in the province of Quebec. The Sûreté du Quebec notified the media of Dayle's testimonies, following which the word spread fast of his new affiliation with the police. Of course, the Hell's Angels caught wind of this and somehow word got back to Dayle that he was now on the Hell's Angel's Black List, a list composed of people who would be eventually eliminated—killed—by active members when the chance arrived. With this news, Dayle became increasingly obsessed about his name being placed on the Black List. He became convinced that he would be killed while in prison. This haunted him daily, and it would be the only thing he would talk about with us when we visited or talked on the telephone.

Again, and again I had to reassure him that his children were safe and so was he. I advised him to consult with prison therapists about his troubling obsession. I am not sure if he saw any professionals, but I am sure he saw a priest; a reflection of his Catholic upbringing as a child, I suppose. But until the murder of my son is resolved and he finally realizes the damage he caused to us, his ex-wife and his own children, I want to stay away. I just want peace.

I sincerely wish that one day members of the Quebec Hell's Angels will read this book. It is my hope that they will find Michael's murderers and teach them a lesson. For if those individuals were trying to gain attention or notoriety as false prospects in their street show towards the Hell's Angels, they made a grievous error in judgement. They killed an innocent young man and put the Hell's Angels at risk of further persecution or investigation by the police. This may deter any future individuals from unjustifiably killing innocent people, and it may protect other parents from the pain that I have had to endure.

And I suppose, in some small way, this may help to release Dayle from his obsession and guilt...

The Hunter's Grim Discovery

Chapter 9

5 November was a beautiful day with warmth from the sunlight. Among all the runner-up stories in 2011, people claimed this year's to be dichotomic weather. Everywhere, growers had faced a very wet spring and a month-long delay to the start of the growing season. Yet their worst enemy turned out to be their best ally when summer weather extended well into the fall, saving what would have been a crop disaster, given the reality of long, often cold and snowy winters in Quebec. We all think in some way that nature owes us a nice summer where she can extend the season until November, but it's hard to believe that two random hunters could suddenly stumble across a mutilated decaying body.

Usually at that time of the year the ground is covered by sumptuous white snow in this majestic province. That day, the clouds in the blue sky were woolly, light and white. I remember going for a walk behind my house, where I could see the black-backed ravens piping on the high branches of the tall pine trees in my driveway. I was hoping that some birds would be already nesting at that time of year and their babies would be fully fledged before the blossoms appeared again upon the leafless fruit trees during the next springtime.

Even if spring was several months away, it was a perfect day to be alive and for huntsmen to catch partridge; it was without a trace of cold. No dandelions were present but the colours of gold, orange and red were still amazing to our eyes. There were no pink flowers on the camellia trees but they were so lovely to behold and think they would bloom in the depths of winter, and by spring they would be old. It was one of those marvellous days in late fall without a chill in the breeze and where a few remaining houses had Halloween sparrows that were chirping on the sunlit garden trees. It would have taken a petulant person to complain about this weather, but despite of such a great weather forecast, this day brought me hell.

Two hunters, a man and his son-in-law, were out walking around dusk along an abandoned railway track that separated a field and the forest along route 173, at Notre-Dame-des-Pins in La Beauce. They were hunting partridges, a common pastime for outdoorsmen in the province of Quebec. Partridges are a vernacular name for several species of birds with similar characteristics. It would be a truly memorable experience for those hunters who went to chase a simple bird. I am sure that day did not end how they thought it would.

To our surprise, many houses were still adorned with skeletons, zombies, crows and other monsters. I would never have imagined that a scarecrow, which looks like a straw puppet planted in the fields to scare the birds from eating sown seeds, would take the appearance of a human.

To my knowledge, scarecrows never entertained a great place in our society. Historically, due to the low value of straw compared to grain, a scarecrow was considered to be an individual of poverty, without financial means or of little or no social importance, unless we admit that this one represented a worthless man, as compared to the person for whom he works, which seems a little far-fetched. Perhaps it comes from a belief that the straw puppet was useful once, that it was used for combat training. It was the one taking the sword in the place of a real person, it would be the one who would have taken the unnecessary risk as part of a simple training, but wouldn't be hurt and would not expose himself, just like the man of straw also allows his sponsor not to expose himself and take risks. Like those murderers who have not revealed themselves or taken the chance to be seen.

It's disturbing when you consider that Michael's body looked like a downed scarecrow when he was discovered in the field by the hunters. From the pictures I saw, and from the way Michael was found, he clearly resembled a strawman. On that afternoon, when the sun was setting over a sunny field where dozens of deer emerge every year, I am convinced that the hunters were expecting a successful hunting trip and they never suspected what was about to surpass their imagination and expectations.

Unfortunately, they are the ones who found Michael's body, and their lives would be forever changed by this tragic discovery on the wonderful day of 5 November on the fields of Notre-Dame-des-Pins, just fifty days before Christmas and fifty-eight days from the first day of his disappearance.

His savagely slain body was discovered a hundred yards away from their house and near the woods, near an enclosure that overlooked the yards.

That day the enclosure was empty, and it was just a day before they started deer-hunting season. A walk along that route through a muddy field has now become an unforgettable spot, an advert now marked with a streamer and plastic flowers to memorialize the death of my son. Even if it is still a bad memory, I still thank God for the fact that they found him, his body, my son.

Approaching the object, they first noticed a foot, thereafter a second one, and then they realized that it was a real human body, covered with multiple insects and worms of all kind and colours. In shock, and disbelieving of what they saw, they ran quickly and hesitantly back to their house where they could inform the police of their ghastly discovery.

In an interview later that week, one of the hunters described the scene: "We ran to our house, the odour was still in our nose, it made us feel really sick." After contacting the police, an officer arrived within twenty minutes. The sun was starting to go down. When the officer arrived, the hunters were still in shock. They told him that they had discovered a dead body.

I wish I knew more on that day what happens when a dead body is found under mysterious circumstances, when it is impossible to establish the deceased's identity or when the cause of the death is unknown. In such situations, we don't even know where to start. Are the police the first to be called? Does it need to be a detective? Or can it be just regular police officer? Do they have the task of calling an ambulance if the person is alive? If the body is dead, do they call a coroner?

On the discovery of my son, the police arrived at dusk, the later part of the twilight period, that time when the sky darkens gradually after sunset when we most commonly like to observe the twilight as it progresses into dusk, where it glows with variable clarity. But in a figurative sense, twilight also means the end of something, the end of life. Sadly, and aptly, it was the end for Michael.

The police officers stayed at the scene for a couple of hours as darkness fell. They took photographs and measured the distance between the body and the train tracks. From altered notes, his body was in an advanced stage of decomposition.

Once the coroner, Mr. Morin, arrived, he transferred the investigation officially to the jurisdiction of the Sûreté du Quebec. He obtained enough information to know that it was a crime and actions needed to be taken toward a criminal investigation. Michael's body was too decomposed for an accurate identity and cause of death needed to be determined.

Mr. Morin placed a call to the local funeral company to collect the body, where it would be immediately transported to the forensic science laboratory in Montreal, about 320km from Notre-Dame-des-Pins.

The hearse owners were from St. Georges, and had been in that business for decades. They claimed that they had never seen so much security involved in transporting a dead body. They were directed by the police to drive directly to Montreal without stopping along the way. Even exhausted from their elongated jaunt, they were not allowed to get out of their vehicle. Michael's decomposed body was removed quickly under the close supervision of two giant security guards. Once his body was confiscated, they closed the murky vehicle door, knocked on the window twice and waved at them to leave immediately.

Instantaneously, Michael's body was placed into one of the horizontal silver refrigeration units in the mortuary. There are no signs of the mortuary in this type of hospital. There are no directions either, but once you make your way down flights of stairs to the basement you discover the undertaker's cases of mysterious death or suspected homicide. These units are secured with a full-size lock and key, only to be opened by the investigators. In all dubious situations, and under tight security, bodies are placed onto trollies which are wheeled to examination rooms for the autopsy to be completed. This is a way of saying that a forensic laboratory is a hospital right through to the end of life. They have to look after the dead, but also, sometimes, the families. It's like being an interim funeral director. They go home exhausted from the physical and mental work, but it's life. Death is a part of life, isn't it?

Knowing that Michael was placed under so much security and was the centre of a criminal investigation was a surreal experience. As I mentioned before, it was like watching a horror movie about my own life.

The Agonizing Wait

Chapter 10

Two days after he was transported to the forensic lab, the pathological process began. This course was an inquest that included an autopsy, which is a physical examination of the body; genetic and toxicological analyses that are collectively used to identify and formulate a cause of death. It appeared to be a very outlandish and lingering process. Minutes and hours seemed like days. This unknown territory looked and felt so much like it did in films, it made it surreal. A few days later, the autopsy gave us details of the crime but not enough elements regarding his identity. For this reason, we were asked to find Michael's dentist. This request was made in order to recover Michael's most recent dental X-rays, which would be used by a forensic odontologist: a specially trained dentist or dental pathologist called upon to recognize his last set of dental records.

The Laboratory of Forensic Science and Medicine in Montreal is an independent service unit of the Department of Legal Affairs in the Province of Quebec. In addition to providing expertise in forensic sciences, it delivers assistance with major crime scene investigations. I was plunged into a real scene out of a horror movie but, and I didn't want to be the lead character anymore.

The centre is responsible for providing necessary legal support and evidence to the Ministry of Public Security, which assists in the continuation of the Ministry's mandate for the protection of the people of the province. So, everything they find is to be held in secrecy. The people of the Forensic Science Laboratory and the funeral homes were an amazing group of people. They were so committed to their jobs and devoted to helping us, but I didn't understand all that clandestineness and silence. His cremation was far from easy, even if we were well informed, and handled in a very discreet manner. With all the respect and dignity nothing was helping to lessen the drama of the grim discovery of his rotten body. To this day, I have the utmost respect for those people. They tackle difficult jobs and provide so much support for us grieving families.

As we went through the horrendous process, the forensics team explained to us the complexity of analyzing Michael's body. The severe stage of decomposition he was discovered in was much more advanced than what is generally expected for a death of this nature and longevity. This was due to Michael's physical stature and the environment in which he was found. That year it was consistently overcast weather which caused the body to decompose more quickly.

The process of decomposition arises as the bacteria and enzymes within the body begin breaking down the body's tissues and cellular structure. For example, enzymes in the pancreas cause the organ to digest itself. A body undergoing decomposition quickly takes on a gruesome appearance, an inflated look; it begins to liquefy and emit gasses such as methane and hydrogen sulfide. These gasses often have an offensive odour due to their sulfur content. Accordingly, this is what the hunters reported as a bad odour coming from the site.

The process of decomposition is accelerated by an increase in temperature, meaning that higher temperatures will cause a body to decompose faster. Likewise, Michael's body was left in a highly acidic environment and decomposed faster than if it was left in a colder environment. The soil composition of Notre-Dame-des-Pins is considered medium-to-high acidity so everything was inclined toward a quick disintegration.

Another consideration is the presence of water, the level of hydration of the body's tissues at the time of death. Michael developed great measures to maintain his health: eating healthy, not smoking cigarettes, and going to the gym to lift weights and do cardio training. He was praised by his friends, both male and female, for his physical stature and dedication to healthy practices. Nutritional supplements were part of his physical training, such as protein powder and recovery drinks. Such supplements are often composed in part with creatine, which helps muscle cells retain more water for improved function. Decomposition of a body is accelerated by the increased levels of cellular and tissue hydration. So, his dedication to nutritional supplementation led to a faster rate of decomposition than would have been expected by an average person.

Within fifteen days, with all the information collected, the autopsy performed and the dental confirmation, the laboratory ruled his death a homicide. From that day onward, Michael's case evolved from a missing person to that of a suspicious death. With additional information obtained during the autopsy, the investigators were able to establish that Michael was murdered late at night, 15 September or early morning 16 September 2011. He died just a couple of hours after I saw him at the Merlin. But here I was alone, fifty-six days later with my own murder mystery to solve, as I review in my head all the unthinkable and awful stories that the newspaper articles reveal, and try to cope with all that BS...

First article that was published by ICI.RADOI CANADA. CA NOV 6, 2011

Two hunters contacted the Sûreté du Quebec (SQ) on Saturday after discovering what looks like human bones in Notre-Dame-des-Pins, Beauce.

According to SQ spokeswoman Ms. G. Bruneau, the two men were hunting partridges when they spotted the bones in a ditch near route 173, near an abandoned railway, after 5:15pm.

The first police arrived at the scene also believed that the bones could be human, but "there is nothing 100% confirmed," said Bruneau.

Investigators were called to the scene to analyse the location and remains. The bones will then be brought to the Forensic Science and Forensic Medicine Laboratory of Montreal, where they will be analyzed.

"If they are indeed human, it will be ruled a suspicious death," said Genevieve Bruneau. "An autopsy will be done to determine the reason for the death and we will check if they are connected to a missing persons file."

Second article

Human bones were found Saturday by hunters in Notre Dame Des Pins, in the La Beauce region.

Ms. G. Bruneau, spokesperson for the Sûreté du Quebec (SQ), explained that the bones were sent to the Forensic Sciences and Forensic Medicine laboratory in Montreal.

They will be analyzed to determine the identity of the person and the exact cause of death. A suspicious death record has been opened.

The SQ is examining the possibility that the bones found in a ditch near the rails of a disused abandoned railway could be those of Michael Carreau.

The 22-yearl-old man disappeared in Saint-Georges, La Beauce, on 8 September.

The relatives of Michael Carreau had organized *battues* at the time to find him, to no avail.

9 November 2011 at 10:48

The human bones found by hunters at the end of last week in Notre Dame Des Pins, La Beauce, were identified by the Sûreté du Quebec (SQ). The remains are those of Michael Carreau, 22, who went missing in St. George on 9 September.

The SQ's Crime Against the Person investigators are asking the public to collaborate in order to trace possible witnesses regarding the death of the young man from Saint-Come, which is considered suspicious.

Ms. A. Mathieu, spokeswoman for the SQ, said that police officers from the SQ Emergency Unit were still on the scene where the bones were found to try to find clues that would be related to the death of Michael Carreau.

The bones were found last Saturday in a dich near an old abandoned railway. They had been sent to the Forensic Science and Forensic Medicine Laboratory in Montreal.

Dozens of police officers participated in the search and investigation. (See pictures.)

Any information may be transmitted confidentially to the central criminal information service 1-800-659-4264.

9 November 2011 at 10:29

The Sûreté du Quebec has identified the human bones found last Saturday in the area of the old railway line in Notre Dame Des Pins. It is Michael Carreau of St. Come, but living in St. Georges. The young man was reported missing 9 September 2011 by family members. The investigators met with the family of the victim in the morning, according SQ spokesman Richard Gagne.

Although we do not know the cause of the death of the latter, the police consider the death of the young man suspect. The investigation was entrusted to the Crimes Against the Person Service.

More than a dozen officers from the SQ participated this morning in a search along the railway line from St. Georges to Notre Dame Des Pins. This search aims to find even more elements that would be left behind to advance the investigation.

Requesting the support of the population, investigators from the SQ's Crime Against the Person department are asking the public to collaborate in order to trace possible witnesses concerning the death of the 22-year-old man.

In order to advance their investigation, the SQ investigators would like to talk to people who met Michael Carreau shortly before his death on or around 9 September.

The autopsy, performed in the days following the discovery of the body, showed that he was a homicide. In addition, information obtained since the beginning of the investigation, and more recently under investigation, has allowed the investigators to establish that Michael Carreau was murdered during the evening of 15 September 2011.

It should be remembered that the man had been reported missing on 1 October, and that he had been found on 5 November in a ditch near the abandoned railway at Notre dame des pins.

The Sûreté du Quebec (SQ) Crime Against the Person Investigation Department is seeking the public's assistance to gather information on the death of Michael Carreau, whose body was found in November 2011 in Notre Dame Des Pins.

The Soothsayers Revelations

Chapter 11

Shortly after Michael's body was discovered, I was desperately seeking answers and I resolved to go visit any extrasensory, spiritualistic or extra supernatural person, whatever the name is, but I was eager for an answer. I really wanted to find out who had taken my child's life. That week I talked with a gentleman on Facebook who was doing enlightening. He explained to me a number of things about enlightenment, and his notion that he thought Michael's spirit was still with us. With regard to my feelings, I could not find a better description than this.

Somebody told me that there was a woman who had the ability to communicate with deceased individuals, and she was excellent at what she did. Despite my disbelieving, cynical and sceptical feelings, I decided to call her and make an appointment.

The day I arrived at her office, it was pleasant outside; again, I recall a beautiful warm yellow house with nice spruce trees and the wonderful colour of the fall leaves. The house was simple and nothing like the other places I visited in the past in La Beauce. I could feel the tranquility; it was so quiet and calm. When I arrived, the psychic was there, and she was a lot younger than I thought. She exuded a beautiful aura and her name was Chantale. I could see pictures of her family on the wall and you could sense that her family was loved and bonded. She politely invited me to her basement and asked me what I was there for. I told her that my son had disappeared and was discovered murdered. I asked her if she could communicate with him and tell me who had hurt him and beat him to death. I aimed to know everything she could divine about this tragedy, this senseless act of violence. Many stories being spread around by people were saying that a girl framed Michael and that he was savagely massacred. I shouldn't believe it, but I remained convinced and was consumed by a fantastical suffering. I aspired to let my pain go. I sensed Michael was still on the Earth and that he should have ascended to Heaven or somewhere. Who knows where we go afterward?

She then invited me to sit on her couch; it was quite comfortable. I asked if Michael was still on Earth or if she knew where he was. I asserted the impression that he had not left the Earth yet. I know it is hard to believe or understand, but I just couldn't put my finger on it. It just transpired to how I felt. She asked a couple of questions, not many, and said Michael is here and he wants permission to sit beside you. I answered yes, and then felt a coolness wash over my skin after she said his name. Up to this moment I had not relayed his name to her. Was it true about her ability? Or had she been informed through the media? I guess I will never know. Then she said something very special, something very unique that Michael did for a long time and that even I couldn't remember as a mother. She said, "Michael wants to lay his head on your tummy like he used to when he was a toddler." Nobody could have known this! How could she know that I or anybody close would not have remembered that? After I affirmed her request, I felt a pressure on my tummy. It was sensational and mostly impossible. She asked Michael all my questions, each time asking permission to talk to him and thanking him for his answers. It was a bizarre way to communicate, but it seemed to accomplish what it set out to do. I suppose by asking permission it summons spirits to talk to the living.

Through Chantale, I asked Michael if he had been killed and his answer was yes. I asked, "How many were there?" He answered, "Three." All this was true and very relevant to the investigation. I asked again; he answered again: "Three." I wanted names and a description of those guys. She then stated that there was a girl and two guys. Immediately, I developed goosebumps all over my body. I asked him if he had suffered. He didn't answer but she said that he had died instantly. I then asked him the names of the murderers again. He refused to tell me and said not to look, but to let the police do their job. The description of three individuals was very interesting. Chantale then revealed that one of the males had a ponytail while the other male was bald. Later, when I discussed my visit with Chantale to the chief investigator, he was dumbfounded. He could not believe it. The police independently had two persons of interest whose physical description matched those described through her.

Michael then reiterated to not look for the killers, that if we were looking for the murderers, we could put our lives in danger. I agreed to his demand. Then she asked me if I was ready to let him go to the universe. Hesitantly, I said yes. I began crying; I couldn't believe what was happening. I was agreeing, "Yes, let go of my son." But at the same time, I knew that I had to let him go to wherever he needed to go. I had to let his spirit go.

I have no idea if it is called a spirit, an enlightenment or God, but I certainly had a bridge that forwarded me the light and the strength I needed. I can honestly say that something astonishing happened to me that day.

For parents who have lost a child, I would say that we never fully recover. Sometimes the ambiguity of our loss makes this experience increasingly more painful, arguably more so if the child has been murdered. Relative to mourning the loss of a friend or older parent, I believe that mourning over the loss of a child is harder because it is a contradiction to the natural repeating cycle of life, where through the passage of time the young inherit from the old. When a child dies, it is incomprehensible for the mother, the one who gave birth. However, fathers can sometimes be more affected, because, due to societal norms and expectations of being "the strong one," they conceal their suffering. There is a tremendous rate of suicide attempts among bereaved fathers. For some fathers it takes longer to once again taste life after the loss of a child and many get throat cancer, which to me indicates that they are unable to yell their pain.

The week after, and in direct opposition to Michael's request, I went to see another soothsayer, Lise, who worked with telepathy, tarot and cards. I was dreadfully looking for his slaughterers. In spite of my doubt of myself as a mother (i.e., I had failed to protect my child), I wanted to identify the assassins. I wanted vengeance. I was determined to find them and march them down to the courthouse. To be honest, I do not think that my thoughts were delivering a dutiful message to my other children. My desire for answers was ingrained too deeply in my consciousness; I would stop at nothing to find the truth.

In hindsight, Lise was very different in comparison to Chantale. I felt she had an ability that complemented Chantal's. Lise could perceive a lot of things that were going to happen in the future. Remarkably, she was able to guess the date of Michael's birth (29 March), tell me that later I would develop a tumour (In 2012: I was diagnosed with breast cancer, had surgery, and everything turned out okay), tell me that I would later find love with a man who would be born in September with a five in his birthdate e.g., 5, 15, or 25; and she said that I would have another daughter in the future, into whom Michael's spirit would be transferred and continue onward.

This daughter would be around thirteen or fourteen years old. When I met my spouse (who was born on 5 September) his daughter was thirteen and she was born the same day as Michael: 29 March. Impossible but true!

In a way, I suppose we all search for happiness and success, and adore the sound of another human's voice telling us that we will one day be financially secure and find endless love. But my visits to the psychics were nothing but trying to reason with death and make sense of my son's murder. But each lugubrious night that life was bringing me had me on my knees commanding God and asking for alms whilst being forced to remain silent against Michael's slayers.

In La Beauce, my mother has for a long time been associated with the paranormal and as a practitioner of Tarot and cards. Using Tarot, my mother is able to communicate with spirits and has done a lot of searching in this domain. After Michael was murdered, she immersed herself in Spiritism as a means to try to find out who killed him. She would often mention to me that Michael was happy, but there were other spirits associated with him that exhibited vicious intentions. We felt as though she had opened a door to an unreal situation.

According to her, "It's easy to summon evil spirits from the paranormal world through cards or others, but it's very hard to get rid of them." Investigators of paranormal phenomena iterate that people can be very naive when they believe they are in contact with the departed souls of their loved ones. They also warn that misuse of these tools can have disastrous consequences.

Unfortunately, my mother did not know how to protect herself from these evil spirits that were associated with Michael's death. Related to this today, my mom is affected with a delirium where she hears disembodied voices, strange noises and projections of voices through the rooms of her house. Sometimes she is unable to function normally, mixing up these voices with real events and now has a hard time putting her thoughts back in order.

My mother was very close to Michael. He loved going to her place and eating her food. My mother and her husband Denis would take time to talk about everything in his life, including cultivation, since she was a good gardener. When he disappeared, my mother had a dream about his death. She woke up that night in tears, saying it was wonderful to see him navigating through the clouds. She mentioned that he was happy in her dream. My mother's visions would sometimes scare me, as they were true all the time. It frightened me to see that everything she would predict would happen.

When Michael was born, my mom was there. That day, my mother had an intuition that I was in mortal danger, possibly dying, and therefore quickly came to the hospital to be at my side. As it turned out, after his birth I was in distress from severe blood loss from my caesarian section and was unable to advise the nurses. When my mother arrived, I was unconscious and lying in a pool of blood. She immediately made the hospital staff aware.

Immediately, I understood that Michael would be special for my mom; I understood that she was to live a love larger than mine. Pure love, true, stronger than anything. She took him in her arms from the bassinette while I was bleeding severely, but seeing her so happy gave me strength which I firmly believed helped my recovery from my complications. That day, I was shaken by a host of emotions I could not put into words. Her eyes contained the same fears as mine. Then, Michael's little hand tried to grab her, as if to say, "Tell mom to hang on, it'll be okay." It was a new adventure for both of us. It was the first time my mother would be present after the birth of one of my children. Both afraid of the unknown. But we already knew that she would love him more than anything, and maybe a little more than the others.

Looking back, I wish, in order to save her from evil spirits and avoid disturbing manifestations, I would have known how to protect her...

Funeral Rituals

Chapter 12

The days leading up to Michael's funeral were far from easy. Not only was I battling the emotional turmoil of losing him, but I had to battle over the funeral arrangements with his father, Robert. I find it ironic how people can change their actions so quickly when it comes to matters of popularity or outward appearance. This is what transpired around Michael's funeral. Literally overnight, Robert went from never-there-dad to full-on-dedicated-dad.

I wanted to have Michael's funeral at St. Georges West Catholic Church, but Robert refused. He continually resisted any of my ideas or involvement and what I wanted for the occasion. Eventually, tired of arguing over minutiae and with little experience organizing funerals, I conceded to let him take care of Michael's funeral. And so, he took the reins, arranging most of the funeral. He had some prior experience, as he had organized his father's funeral a couple of years before.

Two days before the funeral, my five remaining children, Robert and I joined at the Presbyteries near the church in St. Georges. We all sat around a large circular table to discuss the event with Father Duval, so he could prepare for his service. During the meeting, we were each asked to say things about Michael. We each took turns, going around the table. We revealed things such as Michael's personality, qualities, likes, friends, strengths and passions.

Father Duval then advised us that time and patience would be needed in the days following for the final preparations for Michael's funeral. He mentioned that it was very important to take time to prepare, so that the service would not turn into a spectacle. Father Duval was a strong believer that, in preparation for a celebration of life, working together as a family could help lessen the emotional impact of the service for the surviving members. When experiencing grief, there is a need for listening, solidarity and friendship. Other advice he gave us was related to the day and time of the service, flowers, length of the service, music and guest list. Other matters we attended to were the meaning of the funeral, the choice of readings, prayer intentions for universal prayer, the Eucharist, audience participation, processions (candles and cross) and other personalized touches.

Michael's funeral was held on Saturday, 19 November, after his body was released by the Forensic Science and Medicine Laboratory. His body was transported back to St. George, where it was incinerated for the funeral ceremony at the L'Assomption Catholic Church in St. Georges East.

The Church was lovely, but not as magnificent as the St-Georges West Church. Like most churches, those in Quebec are adorned with beautiful murals and imagery, stained-glass windows and elegant woodwork. On that day I was the first of our family to arrive at the church, which was packed with people from all over the region. Father Duval presided over the ceremony. His service was beautiful yet simple. Michael would have preferred it that way; he wasn't one for fuss.

As the ceremony began, Father Duval noticed that a large group of young people were sitting at the back of the church. Father Duval knew of Michael's altruistic nature and recognized that these were all of Michael's friends. I recall one of Michael's closest friends, Emilie, the girl closest to his apartment complex, wrote him a touching letter that she read to those in attendance. She talked about many things: his generosity, his friendship and his love. But what stood out for me was her disclosure of Michael's firm belief in the strength gained from family and friends. This is a transcription of Emilie's letter which I kept for seven years and am unable to read. It is still as painful since Michael's funeral ceremony:

> Michael our friend, our brother. Life has decided to take you too soon. You grew up in the flower of your age; breathing pure air deeply, excreting the torrents of water of a river by strongly covering the effects of a nature to which you were deeply connected. We will always be able to feel your soul: to warm us, to support us, and to watch over us as you have done so well during your life. Your honest, warm, and human laugh. Your humor, your look on life. You were always optimistic, hopeful and passionate. You did that and much more. I do not have words to tell you, the emptiness I feel in my heart and all those who loved you even more deeply. For all the times we had to see over each other without ever judging ourselves. You brought

me to reason when I was lost every time, many times laughing at each other. Sometimes crying with each other.

Your immense joy of life which still characterizes you. I know that now with your beautiful big white wings you will reach higher and nearer the sun. There is so much that I should have told you, making you understand how good a person you were. It was natural to confide in you. You who knew me better than myself. You had this gift. People felt good with you. I think that with your magician's eyes you saw the potential in each of us. What made you happy was to make the people you loved smile. It was so important for me to see you every day. You were an important pillar in my life. It is hard to accept that you're no longer here.

I know that with all the love you felt, you were proud and happy. All your teasing that made you so fond of playing with my guitar. Every time you came to see me you were so happy. You transformed all my flaws, offering me the strength to overcome my fears. The positive man that you were, will be missed, for the rest of my life. With your departure, I have learnt to believe and live my dreams, and to achieve my goals. So, take ease in the trials that happen in your life and come out stronger. You were always a loyal and caring person. You would never leave without making us smile.

Under our tears for those of us who are grieving. Now begins a new era, where we will have to learn to live without you. But the memories with you, will not be easily forgotten. Do you remember the afternoon you returned from fishing, then prepared us a meal of trout breaded with the rice-crispies? All our moments, memories, years together.

I will always think of you, your friend and your almost sister... Emilie.

After that reading, Father Duval noticed that Michael's friends were still sitting at the back and insisted that they advance to the front and pour holy water on his urn. It was so touching. To see them one by one, each of his faithful friends walking hesitantly and slowly to his urn, crying at his loss. Every single one of them on their way back stopped and gave me a hug of comfort before they returned to their seats in the back. Again, for me this was affirmation of Michael's character: love and friendship. To this day I am still very touched by their gesture. It is such a wonderful souvenir.

Michael's father held judgment towards his friends, thinking they were involved in drugs and crime. Some of them used to smoke marijuana, but in my opinion that doesn't make a person a criminal. This was amplified by my fight with him to permit Michael's friends to attend the ceremony. Eventually, he begrudgingly agreed. All his friends have become successful young adults and at that time were only experiencing life.

Sarah, Michael's former girlfriend, sang beautiful songs at the ceremony. She also composed him a song entitled "Pas Seulement pour Moi," which translates to "Not Only for Me." Sarah's mother played the piano while Sarah gave an emotional rendition of her special songs. It was remarkable. Since that time, Sarah has turned out to be an exceptionally popular singer in the province of Quebec as a folk artist, winning many titles and awards throughout *La Belle Province de Quebec*. We then drove to Saint–Jacques-de-Leeds where a dinner was served, and his ashes buried.

After a fatality, family events become so different. Initially it is hard to control your emotions, making assemblies and gatherings difficult. The constant injustice challenges your spirituality and emotions. Desperately, you try to cope with your loss. For many days I attempted to validate his loss, but I knew grieving would take time, and to work with anger and recognize that the death of my son, regardless of the circumstances, was simply horrendous. I strived many times to be compassionate with my friends, groups or family, but nothing was abetting my sorrow. I had little control over a lot of things; I was just not ready for such an ambiguous loss, even if Michael's memorial rituals were meaningless. The fact he was mutilated to death took control over everything; it made me sick. What I couldn't understand, and still don't, is that people who were not very present in Michael's life and were so mean to him were now looking for stardom.

Coping with all those hypocritical people did not make sense to me, but I guess I had to do whatever I needed to do to get through that period of my life.

Insurmountable Emptiness

Chapter 13

Following the funeral, my day-to-day functioning was adequate. I began spending a lot of time in my bedroom, isolating myself from people. I think this marked the period I went from grieving to anger... an anger created by the fact that someone or some people had taken such a good, young life from me. I would spend hours staring dully out of my bedroom window and at the ceiling. I was becoming increasingly vocal and short-tempered. I was expressively telling people to stay away from me, as I no longer wanted to hear sympathy from anyone. As the days progressed, the media became increasingly hostile in their writing, helping spread gossip throughout the community regarding Michael's death. At that time, I sincerely wished that social media, communications and journalism did not exist. I wished they would leave me, my family and Michael alone. From my point of view, we as a society have become partially desensitized by the media. To some degree, we are no longer the same community of citizens that comes together during times of crisis. We as individuals have become, or are drilled to become, automatons without feelings. I find it very troubling how outsiders instantly form hurtful rumors and theories regarding other's tragedies or misfortunes. They in many cases believe everything that is posted on Facebook or in a newspaper, without considering the victims or their families.

For many weeks I lost track of the hours in the day, and the days of the week. One day I awoke to realize that the spruces I had felled earlier were covered with stunning white snow. I was reminded that it would be the cold of winter soon. I wanted to skip that season, and was already anticipating spring, the day when flowers would bloom and I could smell their perfume. I longed for the mornings when I could hear birds sing and see the majestic deer come into my lovely backyard to forage for food. I longed to remember how good life was, but without my indescribable pain. I longed to miss winter because Michael's twenty-third birthday would be in March, and he would remain absent. I recollect so many days and nights where I would sit gazing at my television, my phone and the screen of my computer. I was on my own, isolated, picturing useless things in my mind, journaling with my soul but everything was still hopelessly black. I would awake after hearing his voice in my dreams, but it was short-lived. I had no clue where it was coming from. Sometimes, as I would glance at the clock, I would realize that I had wasted a greater part of my day staring at the darkness of my computer monitor, watching the reflection of the flashing Christmas lights. I would constantly ask myself, "How can I have Christmas when everything has changed? Christmas without Michael?" I was trying to find something to give people as a gift that would help them remember him, so I went to the photocopy store and printed a picture of Michael on his concluding 22nd birthday. When family members would visit, we would sit through moments of silence looking at him, still not believing that he was gone.

From that moment onwards I started hating winter. For many years, I loved it, especially all the fun activities we would do in the snow and on the ice. I used to love the holiday season so much in December. Celebrating with my friends and family, hearing the Christmas carols. Winter also held a special place for me because it is the time of year when I celebrate my birthday. But this year I would turn forty-six without my son. Christmas is always a great feast for everyone in Quebec. I memorized the food and joy at Dayle's place, including my mom's yummy turkey and her delicious meat pies, not to mention all the desserts we concocted such as maple sugar pie and the classic Christmas log from Vachon bakery in la Beauce. The rigodons and bustles for everyone…

But that year the celebrations that are supposed to put a smile on your face would not be the same. We undertook a small gathering with immediate family, wishing for the years to come to be better, when once again we could return to our large celebrations with friends and extended family members. During these subsequent festivities, rather than cry about Michael's absence, we honoured his memory with a toast.

I do not know why, but in Quebec we usually receive an abundance of snow during the holidays, but that year we didn't. It was cold and icy. People practice a lot of things, like our national sport, hockey. I love hockey and miss seeing my son Yohann play. He was such a good player. Cross-country and alpine skiing is a must on our little hills. I still love ice skating, so good for the soul. But once again I was longing for spring, the latter part of the season, the time of year when I can visit any of the sugar shacks with our delicious maple syrup accompanied by its unforgettable smell. In short, everyone can find at least one winter activity that they like. But for me I just wanted to forget time.

I remember when some of us would complain about the cold or do activities outside during winter. Mick would say, "Here is a solution: dress more warmly!" Every year I would be looking forward to November when winter would finally start again. But this is no longer the case, since that is the month, they found his body. I suppose I was lucky that they found him. I have closure in that regard, not driven to search anymore. Some parents never have that chance. I now prefer the sunshine and the heat waves of summer, where I can contemplate the stars lying on the grass and think of him.

Michael's death affected me in many other ways. For many years I stopped taking group family photographs, since his absence would bring me to tears. I could not visit so many places because they were associated with him. There were songs I could not listen to, letters of his friends that I could not muster the courage to read—they all reminded me of him and how good it felt to be around him. But despite this, I wished I could visit his grave more often, but St–Jacques de Leeds was a bit too far for me to go every day.

I kept a journal, which I would write in every day, but sometimes I could barely read what I had written as tears were streaming down my face and soaking the paper. Writing always meant a lot to me, and for so many years I wondered whether this too collapsed along with so much else.

For a long time, my son Yohann thought he would never get his mom back from her despair. If anyone saw me as distant, it was him. If anyone saw me walking circles in my house and in my backyard, they would have thought I was crazy. Many times, we would be traveling to a destination, but I would direct my car in another direction. Yohann would always be at my side, kindly taking care of me, patiently telling me, "Mom, where are you going? You took the wrong road, you have to go the other way." Then we would start laughing our heads off at my absent memory, repeating whimsically, "Mom, where are you going? You took the wrong road, you have to go the other way."

He would always come to my bed in the morning to make sure I was still alive and say, "Good morning, mom. You want to come for breakfast?" So many times, he would cheer me up and give me the strength to continue. Seeing his beautiful smile and how he was strong even at the young age of 12 made me realize that he would have carried the whole world for me. I was so blessed to have him. He would take care of his sister, explaining to her that "Mom is just sad and is going to be okay." He would often cook dinner and put her to bed even if he was destroyed by this loss as well. Michael was his big brother and replaced a dad that was not present in his life. I think they both had that bond and could understand each other.

From time to time, I recall reinforcement visits from friends and family. With the best interests at heart, and to their praise, they were trying to help me cope. But in all honesty, I found these social visits inadequate. I would park myself in front of the counter, listening to mundane words, all affixed with an insincere grin. Again, they would try to reassure me, cheer me up: "You are not alone." But it was not beneficial. For me, they couldn't possibly understand this. How might they? After his disappearance, we had the same conversations but nobody believed me that he was gone. None of them had lost a child to a murder.

I fathomed that my isolation and loneliness could only be shared with others who had the same experience. I needed to reach out to discover parents with identical circumstances. After days of searching, I found the *Association des Familles d'Enfants Assassinés et Disparus* (AFPAD), a non-profit organization in the province of Quebec. Life no longer had the same meaning for me, but this organization was there for those families and parents who have suffered the disappearance of a child, or who have experienced the murder of their child or children. When I found AFPAD, I was hiding and emotionally exhausted. I could barely confess all the trouble and pain that this event had provoked in me. I needed someone to share my story with, others who really understood my anguish. Finally, with assistance from AFPAD, I began to see that I was not alone. There were lists of families who had lost their children. Importantly, this allowed me to realize that I was no longer unaided, no longer isolated, that there were others out there just like me. Even if this realization was extremely soothing, I continued to hide. I didn't pursue any meetings. I just wanted to be alone and I was shy of my anger.

A couple of months after Michael's death, in St-Romain, Quebec, a woman lost her mother and two daughters, all killed by her brother. What I gained and remember from that story was this superwoman's ability to move forward. It was not about the number of deaths in her family but how she handled the situation. How strong she as a mother, who lost two out of four children, was in her ability to come to terms with her loss, and how she was able to control her fears and emotions from the media.

This woman had been a good person all her life, a good mother and a good employee. She was a nurse who worked in a psychiatric ward. She understood the issues of mental illness. Outside of her work, she took care of her brother, who was schizophrenic.

To this day, I still wonder who her gurus were, and what the spiritual practices were that helped her forgive and heal. Was it her understanding of mental illness that allowed her to move on after all those deaths? How to accept the magnitude of this triple murder? I do not know. But for me, she stood out as a beacon of strength and hope. I could barely move, think or laugh after Michael's death. She was interviewed a few weeks after the murders by journalists at her house. She had a face that glowed, she was smiling, her whole demeanor suffused with joy. She was uplifting, an incredible inspiration. That's why, I guess, some people have much more pain than us but overcome it. Because pain is something that can be overcome!

A Lingering Fear

Chapter 14

Later on, with all the rumours of a revenge killing still circulating, I started to become fearful for my own life and the lives of my children. I began to wonder if Michael had been killed for such purposes and if possibly my family would be the next target. This fear was unsubstantiated, but at that time, with my mind set and all the rumors with the Hell's Angels, I developed a farfetched fear of death. I was frazzled, worried for all our lives.

This fear began to invade my whole being, sticking to my skin and becoming impossible to control. Finally, I felt as if I were not living, barely existing, surviving day to day, hour to hour. My mind raced with scenarios of how we might meet our demise. Every minute had become a challenge to keep my sanity.

Sometimes, I would walk hesitatingly to my house because I was scared that somebody was lurking in the shadows, ready to ambush us. There were so many questions about Michael's death, but nobody could give me an answer. Was it because my brother became an informant against the Hell's Angels? Was it because Michael was doing things with his best friend and he wouldn't tell me? Were their other parties involved whom we were unaware of? Or was it because he had been framed by a profiteer who could not pay his debts?"

We have to endure and conquer, if we are to be qualified to help others struggling with similar experiences to ours. My suffering will not have been in vain, if my story helps to ease the suffering of other parents who have lost a child. At times, we convince ourselves that our suffering is worse than that of others, but we should not dispute the suffering of others, since suffering is unique to all of us. And, as I legitimately discovered; there are others whose suffering is worse i.e.: parents whom have lost more than one child.

We do not suffer alone, we always suffer alongside others who suffer (sympathetically) in response to our sufferance. Can we be reborn after our suffering? No, but we can transform wounds into strength. To reduce our suffering, we must distinguish between the pain; real or psychosomatic, i.e. actual physical pain, or pain arising from, all the emotional reactions that can intensify suffering.

To a certain point, I believe that to be happy, we must have suffered to the same extent. Only after we have become aware of our suffering; then can we begin to transform it into happiness. For those who are scared of suffering, are they already suffering from what they fear. Once we acknowledge our suffering, then can overcome it; and find peace. Those who do not know how to bear suffering, will find it's burden more draining than those who do…Those who know how to suffer, can dare anything.

I hope that one day all the difficulties and suffering that I have crossed will be pearls, even if tragedy has mowed me down and death took twenty-two years of his life away. This excruciating ache feels some days like another pain crucifying my suffering heart.

He was commencing to live his dream life but the road of death spent it. An atrocious destiny has hit my lovely soldier and has left me lost for too many years; my only desire is to see the killers in burning fire. Will my spectrum of devotion survive or be destroyed again in that wildfire?

If anybody with a spectroscope could answer, would it revamp my entreaty to God? I was left in such despair, my existence in such desolation, with only God himself to share my pain.

Even if Michael's hazy image appears in my lonely soul as the years are cumulating in my thoughts, all these blurred images, distorted from these past joys and of this existence, on which the curtain fell like a horror scene, all will never be closed. And with all the distant voices resonating in my heart, I continue to hear his voice at certain minutes and hours of the day, even after it has been silent for several days. This cruel destiny leaves behind an overexposed image that does not belong in my head. Like the dark nights that came after Michael's departure, now I know how to emphaticize and soften it by the love that connects me to him. Beyond what is known or visible, I still and will always question myself as to where he is or what really happened to him.

I remember one night in particular. Kelly-Ann, who was nine years old at the time, was nestled in bed beside me, fast asleep. Yohann was sleeping in his bedroom in the basement. As I watched the deer rummaging through my front yard, I heard a noise coming from the front of my house. The noise came from the driveway. To my surprise, there was a car parked at the entrance to my property. I could see a man sitting in the car. He was looking at something, like a document. It was dark; I could barely see. Then he got out of his car, and went to his trunk to retrieve something. My heart began to race; I could hardly breathe. I truly thought someone or some people were here to kill us all in our house as we slept. I did not know what was happening. I was thinking the worst. Was it a gun? A bat? I scrambled away from the window to call the police, explaining to them that there was noise around my house and a man sitting in a car in my driveway. I was so scared, my whole body was shaking, and my teeth were chattering in my mouth. My body was inert and I could barely move. At that time, I used to sleep with a big hammer beside my bed. I was ready to hit anyone who posed a danger to me or my children.

After several minutes, I was directed immediately to an officer and talked to them the whole time they were driving to my house. My legs were quivering so badly I could barely walk. When the police arrived, the man was still in the car. Fortunately, it turned out to be a lost traveller, seeking a place to park to check his road map. It is uncanny how your imagination can play tricks on you!

I suffered for months as my fear of death turned into anxiety. An anxiety that restricted my social function. But where was my anxiety coming from? For days, I remember going to my children's room very early every morning to check that they were still alive, breathing, moving, to see that they were still in their beds and to ensure that nobody had forced my door or my windows. I would repeatedly check for footprints in the snow around my house, or tire tracks of cars in the fresh snow on the drive way. I was scared to go outside by myself. It had become like a poison and I was fearing that something bad could happen and my subconscious was predicting another murder for the future.

Like an animal, I was fearing immediate danger, which happens most of the time in the present moment. But humans are the only species who can be afraid of what *could* happen, scared of things that are not happening at the moment. We fear the worst in our consciousness. This fear, as some people say, is necessary: It prevents us from doing stupid things. But I finally find that most of these fears are useless, unfounded, and can prevent us from moving forward.

For months, my fear of death and being killed by the Hell's Angels remained unmanageable. I focused on everything that said "Hell's Angels": clothes, pictures, reports on television, newspapers. I lived in a tribe with a belligerent God of battles, it was like being in Hell with Satan. I was coexisting with the Hell's Angels, harbouring dark thoughts all the time, I was so convinced that I was going to be touched by death again. And asking myself: Who wins against the rival tribes? I was urging for peace and harmony. I also shuddered upon hearing words related to them, death or to a cemetery. I was causing anguish to myself and everything and everyone, whether near or far. It was unshakably making myself believe that I would die. It was fashioning into death. So, I managed to avoid direct confrontations with what had become a phobia.

So, to clear my mind, I went downtown and spoke to a couple of guys who were directly affiliated with the Hell's Angles. I inquired as to whether my son owed money, or if in any way he was involved in something with them. My contact was a close friend of my brother's and he had been sympathizing a lot with the Hell's Angels. He confirmed that Michael had nothing to do with them, but he was sure that he was framed by a girl who owed money and that he was sent to do something for someone else and that person omitted telling him that she was in trouble with them. The police still think that this is the strongest theory.

Later on, I would listen to the media, and every tragic disappearance or murder of every young child replenished my fear once again. The mental barrier that I had weakly built to face my fear was eroded each time I heard of another child abduction or disappearance. For me, this is the most heart-wrenching aspect of all. Not only that we have to deal with that anxiety, but to worry over the fate of the missing is not understandable. Even if mine lasted only for a short while, it seemed like the months were years.

But after those months, I was able to tame my anxiety with help from Johnny and the children. Looking back, those were very long days. I would not wish those feelings upon my worst enemy, as the saying goes.

Digging for Suspects

Chapter 15

Avoidance was a strategy that I used for a short period of time. When going into town, I would change sidewalks to avoid seeing people I knew. By limiting my contact with others to reduce the crackle of propaganda, I began to accept that my life would be a skin of sorrow. This, with my fear of death, was preventing me from the joy that life has to offer. It was as if I had a cancer in my mind: anxiety, fear, sadness, creating a meagre existence from day to day.

Fortunately, after months of avoidance, I had an epiphany. I had to change this trap for myself, and for my children. To tackle this problem, I decided to start therapy with a psychologist. My goal was simply to make sure I could live with my fear *and* accept the death of my son. After many sessions, I slowly began to realize that I was not a unique case. This first bit of good news revealed that many people suffer from the same fear as I did, especially after a murder. To my surprise, the fear was a normal part of the grieving process encountered when a family member has been murdered. The only downside to this was that there was no quick, easy remedy for my fear. I knew that it would be a long road to recovery.

Over time, reassurance from the psychologist helped me gain confidence back in myself as a mother. In turn, it helped me to begin relaxing again, and allowed me to refocus and learn how to manage my dark thoughts and the turmoil in my mind. As part of this process, the therapist gave me two tasks. The first was to create a list of all the situations that annoyed me. This list was composed at my own pace and was for the purpose of learning to control emotions. With each situation, I had to step back to observe as a third party, determining if the situation really had any true bearing on my life or my children. For example: I would get frustrated when someone would cut me off in traffic. By analyzing this situation and my emotional response, I was able to determine that this small situation did not have any real impact in my life. Thus, by learning to control my emotions on these little situations, I could eventually apply this to tackling my big situation—my anxiety and fear of death.

The second task that the psychologist asked me to do was to compose a list of people who I thought were involved with Michael's murder, i.e., a list of suspects. As I created my compilation through word of mouth and social media, I would categorize and write items regarding each person. In my small journal, I placed suspect's names on the right-hand side of the page, and any or all comments and pertinent information of the left-hand side. I found that my research, my reading, and documenting in this manner helped me to understand and organize my thoughts. I endeavored to hide my workbook from the eyes of everyone, since I feared the list could be found by those who killed Michael. I was still fearing the worst.

Michael's best friend (MBF) was my first suspect. I think MBF was a very good influence for Michael, but for a long time I thought he was one of the murderers. I know that he went to the apartment, texted and called Michael several times that night. For all sorts of reasons, through thick and thin, I still have him on my list. I do not believe that he killed him, but I am convinced that he knows who did. MBF helped Michael several times financially, so I think that he was exchanging favours for something. People were saying that MBF was selling cannabis and wanted Michael to sell for him. MBF did not have that profile and would often mention to me that Michael was like a little brother to him. I know that they both liked to smoke cannabis and grow different varieties for their own recreational use. It was more like a challenge between them to see which one cultivated a crop with the best flavour. Michael was really thrilled by the idea that marijuana could grow in different flavours.

MBF was living in the same little town as me: St-Come, Linière. It was a lovely place to live and raise a family. People would gather regularly, like one big family. St-Côme had all the amenities that one would need. Everything was accessible by walking, and it was without the need of waiting for cashiers at any of its shops and markets. The town had an amazing grocery store filled with delicious hot and cold meats. It also had a large bakery—it started as the Bakery Doyon—where they produced varieties of breads and many other pastries.

Although in the same town, MBF was difficult to locate after Michael's death. Michael had him in his personal telephone list, as he called it: "my little black book." In its entirety, it took me five days to find MBF. The reason I wanted to contact him so much was to enquire about all the missed phone calls and texts he left on Michael's cellphone. I knew that he wanted to see Michael that night for something, but I had no idea why there were so many calls. What was he looking for? MBF's cellphone was bought with pay cards, and had no real name registered to it, but a fabricated name instead. We had proof that this number was the last communication on Michael's cellphone, just a couple of hours before his death. The search for MBF involved days of immersion in Facebook, reading profiles and viewing personal photos of friends. After I managed to locate MBF's profile, I noticed that he had a new tattoo on his back. I surmised that if I could find the artist who did the tattoo, I would possibly be able to track down a contact person or MBF, and a new address or cellphone number. The new generation always gives out their phone numbers to tattoo shops, as they crave their artwork.

I was determined to find this number, to find MBF. As painful as it was, I knew it would help me in my course of healing. I needed to know the manner in which he was killed. I hoped that visualizing would help me fill in most of the blanks and answer my burning question that was haunting me: Had he suffered before his death? If so, for how long? Or was it an instant death, passing quickly?

The first place I visited in my search was the tattoo shop on 1st Avenue in St-Georges, La Beauce. It was one of the most popular shops in the town and was often host to my brothers, Dayle and Johnny. I still think that Michael was guiding me through my search, since this, as it turns out, was the only shop that I needed to visit. When I entered, I asked the owner if he or one of his artists had created the tattoo for MBF. With Michael's brutal departure, reality was suddenly turning into a nightmare, leaving me extremely anxious, sweating and shaking like never before. Nevertheless, to face the terrible truth was better than to deny it.

I remember arriving there that afternoon like it was yesterday. When I entered the shop, the girl at the front desk asked me why I was there. I told her that I needed to see the owner of the tattoo parlor. I knew him well, he was a much-respected tattoo artist, known for his amazing work. Usually, people in the drug industry that do something memorable have a tattoo done shortly after, as if it were a ritual, especially for gang members or those trying to become a member. I was convinced that the tattoo on MBF's back would lead me directly to him, and to the mysterious phone number. As is generally known, people hiding the truth from others usually have signs that we can recognize at a glance. Shifty eyes, croaky voices, sweaty palms are all detectable signs that someone is lying. That owner had none of these signs, as he had nothing to hide. He gave me all the information but was careful answering my questions, since he knew who I was. The important thing is that I managed to obtain MBF's cellphone number. When I confirmed MBF's name and number in the registry book, I started crying. I ran outside to my car. I sat in silence inside my car. I felt relieved but horrified. I was guided to one of Michael's buddies. Not only were tears rolling down my face, but my legs were shaking. I had the worst feeling inside my soul. I could not believe the possibility that Michael's best friend, who had come personally to my house, could be the slayer. I was sure that I had found the killer; I was convinced it was him, someone he knew or someone he was with.

I subsequently drove to the police station to forward this information to the investigators. When I arrived, I was seated in an interrogation room. I was bit confused; I was trying to find Michael's atrocious murderers, yet I was being interrogated? Constable Couture and his partner came into the room, greeting my warmly and courteously. What I had discovered was very troubling to me—could MBF be involved with Michael's murder?

I learned from the investigators that MBF had been previously located and taken to the station for questioning. As it turns out, MBF was supposed to meet Michael on the night of his disappearance. According to MBF, Michael had failed to show up at the bar later that night. MBF had shown the police all his texting history, revealing Michael's absence and MBF's alibi, the people who were with him for the entirety of the night. With this new information, the police had to dismiss MBF as a suspect in Michael's murder, and no further accusations could be made against him.

Even with this information, my perspective remained unchanged. I still felt MBF was related to Michael's murder. I wish I could be forgiven for feeling this way. Later, I was informed that sometimes, on rare occasions, the Hell's Angels would mess with families in response to a snitch. That they do kill the families and the main objective is to monopolize the family to make the snitcher abandon his lawsuit or cease further disclosure. I thought this was irrelevant in my case and a strange way to support their brothers. Later on, you realize that the enemy of our enemies is our friend. So maybe it was MBF? He spent a lot of time sympathizing, and buying a lot of items for my son. My viewpoint today: I find him hypocritical, as he could not be genuine about his actions which imply, he prefers escaping the truth about Michael's death. He has always been my first suspect and still is. He was also the last one in contact with Michael and the scenario of his death is quite troubling in my mind. Maybe he had to work with an enemy and sent Michael to wash his dirty clothes. When I recently (2018) asked the police about MBF and if whether he was still a suspect, the investigator said he wouldn't answer my question. I find this very troubling. Given this, I will never relinquish the idea that it could be him, his best friend.

As I continued with my list of suspects; with each stage crossed and each name eliminated, I realized through this that nothing serious would happen to me or my children. In fact, I began to find it easier to speak about Michael's death. Moreover, my outlook on death, or rather, my fear of death began to change. On one occasion, while I was writing in my journal, I wrote: "I will eventually die one day." This helped me realize that death was inevitable. In the present, I was not dead, I was alive. That argument seems not very persuasive, but such an idea was helping me feel better. I had to continue to live. I diverged from the point of existing to the point of thriving. It would be the way Michael would want me to continue. When this came about, I decided to reduce my search and start moving forward.

Realizing that life and death intermingled, I discovered, with my friends and my family, that cemeteries were soothing places, where we can relax and rejoice. I also discovered that what was written on the stone is not very important, even though I still have anger that my name is not written on my child's stone, as Michael was buried in Robert and his wife's plot. I couldn't afford such an expense, as I never expected it to happen so fast and drastically; but I know in my heart, Michael and I shared a deep connection with will transcend time.

Today, after seven years of self-help therapy, I can say that I have overcome my anger. Taming and accepting death has helped me to enjoy life more. Before, I brooded over the past and I was anxious for the future, which left me no room for the present. Today, I have come to terms with Michael's death, and I understand that I had to let go of him to accept the unacceptable. "As far as the present is concerned: I live one day at a time, making the most of every moment with my new rebuilt family."

Coping with Grief

Chapter 16

There is no pill strong enough to ease this agonizing pain or no intelligent book which you can read to teach you how to grieve. Like parenting, grieving is singular and dreadfully unique for each person. You have to battle arduously and try to crawl your way through, to continue on with your own life. And I really mean try, as each day we are devastated, merely existing. In some way, we always remain with an excruciating grief, albeit with less intensity some days.

If you are currently grieving as such or you know or think you know what it is, I would embolden you to glance at the following few chapters. It is with my saddened heart and my enormous hope that by telling you my hurtful journey, you may be able to glean some points which can help you in some way to aid you in your recovery from your loss.

The process of grieving can be found in numerous psychology offices painted in delightful murals, best-selling textbooks or the infinite online grid. Generally, grieving can be broken down into steps that each person traverses. These stages are atypical and happen at diverse times. They are: denial, anger, bargaining, depression and acceptance. In reality, these phases *are far from easy* and are not so cut and dried; there is no clear demarcation how to climb between the scaffolds. Likewise, we may encounter many of these junctures at once, in distinctives combinations, and with assorted lengths of time. As for myself, and as you may have seen in earlier chapters, I stumbled at every single step, at various times of the day, in the months and in the years. Even today, I am still tormented by the actions of his unidentified assassins.

Even if Michael was twenty-two years old, he was still my little boy. Other parents who have experienced the same loss often say the same thing. They are still our babies and always will be. With our young adult's departure, we have a lack of support, due simply to the bond that still exists between the grown child and the parent. Whatever the reasons are, for the parents the grief is the same—it is inconsolable.

The fact that Michael had been murdered was a gruelling, strenuous and an unfair circumstance. People are senseless, judgemental and irrational. You became almost criminal-like in their eyes. They do not understand the families, and that we had nothing to do with the crime. They fail to recognize us as victims. You become naked in front of everyone and they are not afraid to take off all the dignity you have left. It's not only that death propels you into mental shock, into uncontrollable emotions and drains you physically all your energy, it also takes a toll on your finances. It is gross negligence of the government that we are not recognized nor covered for our loss. Dealing with other people becomes complicated. The doubt, fear and anger that inhabits you lingers for an exceptionally long time. Frankly, I lost faith and trust in other people. And, I became so vulnerable that I was almost not able to support my own life, let alone sustaining the life of my other children.

When death occurs in an ultimate tragedy, nothing is more devastating. Along with the usual symptoms and stages of grief, many issues surrounding the murder and the disappearance make parental bereavement particularly difficult to resolve.

Feelings of injustice are common, but easily understood by others. More often that not, we have a feeling that this murder "should never have taken place." The excruciating pain alternating with numbness is a dichotomy that may persist for months or longer. You feel that you can merely exist, and every motion or need beyond that seems nearly impossible. It has been said that coping with the loss of a child requires some of the hardest work we will ever have to do.

I think the relationship between parents and their children is among the most intense in life. Much of our parenting centres on providing and doing for our children, even after they have grown up and left home. A child's death robs you of the ability to carry out your parenting role as you have imagined it, as it is supposed to be. You feel an overwhelming sense of failure for no longer being able to care for or protect your child; duties that you expected to fulfill for several years are now vanished.

I find this awfully unfair. Feelings of insecurity and powerlessness overwhelm you. Some days, you would like to just go home, have a drink to feel better and tell yourself that it will be over tomorrow. There are days where no medicine is strong enough to ease your pain, and you feel like giving up on your own life. This part of the grieving process was incredibly perplexing for me.

Initially for a short time, I firmly believed in my consciousness that he was still here, and that he was taken somewhere. I suppose, it was like refusing death, especially since I did not identify his body. You hopelessly think that there is a chance that either our consciousness carries on in some non-observable form or it's just, well, in your mind that he may not be gone. I knew from the bottom of my heart that nobody could answer my questions, and that I was left alone with a big hole in my soul. I remain here on Earth, inflected with basically no courage to know where to sit in all of this.

I began thinking about the two of us reunited somewhere and came up with a neat little hypothesis, but I'm not sure how we can test its validity. My thought is that there is an existence of a field of consciousnesses that resonates throughout the universe, just like a large magnetic field. One day, somebody will create an event that essentially reunites your consciousnesses together. Of course, this may philosophical nothingness, but interesting stuff to think about, but unfortunately, it would not answer any of my questions.

I spent days stuck in anger, and I hope nobody blames me for that. I had so much bitterness and revenge in my heart. But eventually, one day, I did manage to lower my rage and reactions. I found a way to consciously choose happier emotions and healthier vitality, to replace my discomfort and melancholy. Yes, in the beginning it feels inconceivable, but I did it and so can you!

I know it feels horrible and you think you cannot see the light at the end of the tunnel. But one day you start thinking about the positive aspects of your child's life—his energy, the light, the pleasure and love that they brought to your life. You realize that you are still alive, and that they would like you to be happy. You have to ask yourself: "How would they like to see me now?"

You have to think that you haven't lost them, but rather, they have changed realms. They have graduated to the other side. And in this place, you will once again see them in the future.

We all deserve to feel overjoyed and peaceful again. Your children, family and friends need your happiness. Your loved one is in a place of peace, light and love. He does not want you to be sad; he would want you to live and remember life, have dynamism and seize each moment. Even if you inaugurate one day at a time, over time it will metamorphose. You will recover and retrieve ways to share all the blessings you have, like your other children, your family, your friends and your own life.

I yearn to know that my son did not suffer as much as I think he did. If somebody could assure me of that and indicate he died quickly, it would comfort me. There are no good reasons to think that he suffered from that experience. I believe that the consciousness of a person disengages from the body just before fatal injury. Medically, it is considered physiological shock. Survivors of near-death experiences have said that, although they were shot, stabbed or had fallen from great heights, it only felt like a punch in slow-motion, and that's it. They say they knew the essence of the event, but not the reality of it. I hope that to be true.

Some days, for me, the colour of the sky has different shades of blue, and sometimes it turns to hues of grey. Some days you watch the beauty of the sky and you hear messages from your deceased loved ones. You imagine them flying back upward into the heavens, opening their wings like beautiful angels where they belong. It is so hard not to lose heart, even if we think that they are with us, that they are living in a parallel universe to ours and that one day we will join them to all be together; it is so hard to guess where it we be.

I think that my son many times breaks through the dimensions and wants to give me messages of hope and love. Every time I have been in need and asked him for help, it seems he made it possible.

I encountered psychologic and physical symptoms during this time: Headaches, neck pain and shoulder pain were the most common manifestations I encountered. A therapist who specializes in post-traumatic psychologic shock explained that this occurs as the result of an increase in mental workload, stress level and cortisol release. I also ended up with a breast tumour six months after his death.

Some days, I reacted like a person with classic antisocial personality disorder, since I had no trust of others or the will to communicate with them. I hated those individuals who exploited and killed my son. And so, I was transposing that hatred to others, those who were innocent and unrelated to his death. I found it challenging to be in society without any trust.

Through this period of my life, I was struggling to maintain relationships with my friends and family. For many days, I wanted to separate myself and could only focus on finding Michael's killers. I had no fear, even if it was to engage myself in activities that were grounds for arrest, including fighting, beating and even killing them all. I even considered taking MMA courses to use against them.

Frequent scenarios of self-revenge followed by anger were in my daily program. I was easily triggered, and if I could meet them, I would have no reservation about violating their physical (human) rights. I would have no remorse because of their behaviour and I cannot believe that people ever rationalize and keep subdued about what they did. It is similar to when I think about my father and all the pain he imposed on with. I'm a hater of those specimens.

People often ask me: How were you able to move forward after experiencing all this? I always tell them how good and kind he was, and that I'm too busy creating another dream and a better life for my love, his brothers, sisters, my grandchildren and for myself. I remind myself as well that he wouldn't want to see me cry over his death, or walk around sad, angry, bitter and drowned in tears. Michael surely would not be proud of his mom if she was any of these. I want him to be proud of me wherever he is. Not that I didn't cry, but there is a moment to build a wall over all those tears.

Today, I remember the things he adored in me. Michael loved my entrepreneurship and my creativity. He wanted to reproduce that talent in cooking and baking. There was nothing better than his bruschetta and brownies. Now when I assemble people around my table, I try to crack a joke that reminds me of him.

Suffering is an enormous part of healing, but when you have ached enough, you finally realize that it is not how your deceased loved one would like to see you, and that *you* are the *only* person who can change that. There is only one person who is completely responsible for your own true happiness—it is you! When you accept that, you will be able to shift your focus and state of mind. This in my opinion is the biggest undertaking you will encounter during your healing process.

From this point onward, you will improve your recovery every day. You will allow yourself to smile again. You take every little thing you see and with all your consciousness perceive it with more love. It is by applying love that we can release our soul from the shackles and the pain to become free again, and to once again feel peace and joy. Experience with death makes us more permeable, more cognizant of the suffering of others. We must share that suffering before reasoning. There is no hurt that sympathy can alleviate, and there is no limit to the tyranny of man, but there will be a limit to the agony that we have to endure.

Although I thank my emotional endurance, I acknowledge that the pain was more resilient than me; she dominated me for extensive periods. She trained me to agonize and threw me against chimeras that hurt me for way too long and made me scream way too loud. I erected neither peace nor security. The worst suffering was the loneliness that accompanied me every second of the day, especially when nobody would believe that Michael was dead.

The determination of the body is little compared to anguish of the heart. Suffering endured sometimes gives us too much assurance; she herself has her vanity. Suffering does not have many friends, but those she has are sincere. A fault which is paid for by suffering weighs less on the delicate conscience than the one which appears unpunished. But if I wanted some way out of my paralyzing wretchedness, I had no choice but to aim for a spiritual goal. I yearned for that happiness, and to obtain my goal I started asking myself *again and again*: "How would Michael like to see me?" I knew that he would like me free from emotional turmoil. Six months after, hour after hour, still in the kitchen reading his forensic medical report and rambling about what I would do. It was very quiet. Nothing in the investigation was happening. I sat for long hours trying to find a solution to ease my guilt. Once again, I received no answers; everything was pitch black. As angry as I was, I began to become angered with the officers of the investigation. It was all very well for them to look so tranquil, and understand or empathize with my grief... but, how could they? I'd like to see them maintain that calm in the face of losing their own child.

I sought people who knew something, but I was not allowed to have any information. I found myself attentively begging for any piece of information that had the slightest relevance. I remained duly chastened. There was hurt everywhere. In how many ways does this sufferance need to be brought to this planet? Once again, I'll go to bed with a sleeping pill, but it won't be effective towards reducing my suffering or my illness. I resume my search and again I'm trapped, looking inside his circle of friends. I tried so many times to avoid this, to stop this, but when you are in an upheaval for two years, five years, and now seven years, it is like a roller coaster of emotions, the silence that governs your days by not finding the assassins brings you down, and you are there incapable of doing anything else.

Now, I take each day and make it a little treasure. I cherish all the little things with my family and start breaking out in tears of laughter rather than sadness. I even laugh about my tears of laughter. Everything gives me strength that I never knew I had or knew existed. Life no longer has the same meaning, happiness is not the same and *I do not* feel guilty about myself anymore. Now, I protect myself from the drama and the ridicule of people.

I do not sit around and wait for the inspectors to find the killers or try to find them myself. I am thoroughly done creating anger and fear. Even though, at times, I find myself getting triggered, lashing out at people, picking fights with my kids or partner. I feel contempt towards them, my friends, coworkers, clients or boss. I have to say that I'm not guilty and can't blame myself for not being able to prevent them from killing him.

I think suffering is caused by an attachment or some kind of nonsense that we hold on to. It can be a positive outcome, a negative one or simply an avoidance of the truth.

I have come to the conclusion that these are patterns and that we are merely in need of letting go. So many individuals have patterns that can interfere with our ability to really let go. There should be psychological exercices to show people how to let go, to help us get rid of the stress and the strong sense of helplessness.

I think the best way to start is to know if we are ready to let go. Have you suffered enough, and do you have the willingness to do so? Sounds simple, but it is so hard. But there is something that we do that makes us hold on to dear life and everything in those cases comes from fear—the fear of losing another kid, fear of losing money, fear of hearing the truth. We are raised to thrive on drama.

Some people really need attention or the power that holding on gives. For a fact, I deal with one every day and the only thing that person loves are the practice of destroying the lives of others. Hard to understand when you look at the portrait of big houses, Vuitton purses, Botox and plastic surgeries, she always had a way to make people lower then herself.

So, when you have an obscure day and feel upset, angry or irritated by others, step back, do not lower yourself to their level, do not feed their misery with your tears or emotions, and at all costs, remove yourself from those who thrive on drama. Above all else, learn forgiveness; forgive your own sins and the sins of others. Every day, love those around you for what they are, not what you want them to be. It is easy to blame others for all that's gone wrong in your life, but it is also very hard to live with the remorse of not having taken the time to forgive.

Preventing My Soul from Being Shattered

Chapter 17

Death rips you apart in many ways, especially if it is caused by a sudden and unnecessary act of violence. Bitterness from this event is very intense and particularly long to remedy. I should have asked for the help I needed, but on the flip-side, without seeking outside help I thought I was protecting myself from further exposure to the media. As far as I am concerned now, the bereaved should not hesitate to consult professionals, since they are able to provide much-needed psychological support and attentive listening for as long as necessary. But I was afraid and lost and thought that people would think I was crazy.

Deeply shaken by the violent death of my dear son, I found it painful to continue moving forward. What good is it to do projects since life is so fragile and death so sudden? The danger is then to lose all confidence in the future. Extremely disillusioned, I shut myself up until I developed bitterness and hardness in the face of existence.

Our bodies, our minds and our souls are so complex. Severe mental distress causes and exacerbates physical symptoms, even if I had the chance to have remarkable dreams about my son. Today those dreams fill me with hope and peace that passes all understanding. Six months after his death, I had to go through another hardship. I had to face the fact that maybe I would go join him. As previously mentioned, I developed a tumour in my breast. Maybe my sorrow was so big that I channelled his pain through my body. I just couldn't let him go. I was stuck in non-acceptance, refusing to bear the burden of his unpredictable death.

It became a double-edged sword. There were inspiring times when I was very positive and optimistic about finding the killers, and I maintained a deep desire inside of me that kept telling me to keep fighting. But at other times, hopefulness was dashing it with contrasting emotions that invaded me deeply, together with despair and turmoil.

I was endlessly oscillating between hope and constant desolation, which made my grieving like a roller coaster. It was stressful and prevented me from finding mental peace, keeping me away from closure. I knew that Mick was killed but not knowing what happened to him had a big effect on my mental health and body.

I was unable to accept the fact that those assholes took him away from me. I do not forget the fact that he had been there in that field, lying there for many hours with all those wounds. I was thinking all the time of what that woman told me, that he was fatally hurt because they beat him to death, breaking almost all the bones in his body, and then enveloped him in a pink fiberglass insulation bag because he was bleeding too much. I can't imagine how much blood he lost. My heart, my body, my soul was feeling every single thing. My neck, my spine, my shoulders, my legs, every part of my body was aching. So many days I was dreaming of him dead, face-first in the ditch.

People say that interpreting a dream can be very subjective. I believe that my dreams spoke for themselves and helped me connect the dots months later. Every night after his landlord called, I was having a hard time falling asleep. I was lying down in my bed; I could hear the sound of the leaves so clearly in my ear. When I managed to fall asleep hours later, I would always have that abstract dream of the separation, the dreams of what my subconscious was telling me, the abstract evidence that I would be separated from my son. He had to leave for a reason, it was telling me, maybe for the love of someone that had been taken away from him, maybe he was suffering from a disease that he was worried about or didn't want to tell. The association wasn't clear. Maybe it was someone who was wanting him to suffer or maybe it was a best friend that he was helping to get out of trouble.

Having someone who is taken away from you doesn't bode well for your future. They say that dreams are reflections of our innermost self and that the thoughts and emotions come via a story to you in your dreams. This forces you to constantly analyze your life and events. Some say, that dreams show your future logically? Possibly?.

How can we see something occurring in a dream and then see it become reality? I think it is called visual perception. It is when the image is formed in your mind, then it takes place in reality.

We all have that common type of dream in which we dream about the death of someone. We are left feeling quite dreadful and it is a terrible feeling to have. In my case, it had a more prolonged impact. My mind was disturbed, left with an irreparable mark. There were lots of indications in my recurring dreams on the death of my son. My mind was reacting and getting all types of clues. I needed that piece of evidence or information in the future for detecting his crime or solving the mystery of his missing body.

I have not yet been able to learn why I was having those dreams. Those dreams eventually turned into reality, since they found his body as I had dreamt it. Many believe that dreaming stems from a protective connection between mother and child. I can certainly agree with this.

After Michael went missing, people were telling me to think positively, to be well, that it was only a dream. They told me to stop putting yourself down with dark thoughts. But now I would argue, to all of those people… I did see the truth. I was not crazy or thinking the worst. I was just having a premonition. I was seeing the future. I was predicting what was going to happen.

There is a direct connection between dreams and signs from the great beyond. Are dreams and signs a technique for our deceased relatives to contact us to let us know they are fine and are indeed living on? I believe in my heart they do. I was fortunate and blessed they found my son. Was I privileged with that dream and to have numerous dreams and signs of my deceased child? Maybe. Although they varied in different contexts, they all did have the same theme. They were communicating that he still exists and that one day we will be together. Just like death and life, grief has no time and neither do signs or dreams. They all come at any time, look all the same and we should always be open to our child who is trying to communicate with us in a dream.

For people to cope with bad dreams and premonitions, there are many mental health professionals who are able to accurately diagnose and provide appropriate help. It is imperative that parents of the victims of violent deaths seek their help. Otherwise, we and our family members remain with lifelong mental damage, unanswered questions and sometimes the over-judgement of people. It is important that we survive with the support and care that we deserve.

I endured hatred and resentment, which I believe in my head made my body sick. Although we parents suffer emotional repercussions long after the immediate physical symptoms, it is the mental impact which, in the long run, becomes so disturbing that our body reflects our subconscious. My breast tumour is a real example. My tumour was located on my body on the same side and was the same size of the blade where Michael's largest and fatal injury was found. I will always remember the first question the oncologist asked me when I sat in her office. She asked me if I had had a shock or a change in my life in the last six months. According to her, some breast tumours are triggered by shock and can develop rapidly. I answered, "Yes, my son was murdered last November." She took a long breath and immediately called the surgeon to have my lump removed as soon as possible. I thank God that this was taken fast enough and removed immediately.

I remember for days I was deliberating on how to deal with my pain, his pain, our pain. I indulge myself only in suffering, I was creating my torment. I wanted reassurance and someone who would tell me the truth, but no, there was nothing, only desolation. The only thing I had to learn is that the silent treatment would only punish me. I was listening to the sound of silence that, like a cancer, could grow and eventually kill me. I was saluting darkness who became my companion to confess to, and the vision of his pain was slowly creeping and planting in my body, and still is...

People can tell you that what you are feeling is normal. You cannot find the answers to your questions right away, even if you do the best you can and have faith that everything is going to be okay. You simply cannot. I do believe with my whole consciousness that life is good but the world is not. We live in a world that has fallen apart, full of pain and with all kinds of sickness. But when emotional grief affects you, you become a stranger to your own body and mind. This is not a purpose for humanity. We are meant to live with no pain, sadness or trouble.

We are taught that in order to be at peace, we need to feel sacrifice. How can the sacrifice of our child be the price to pay for our own peace? Isn't that the wrong price? It is so hard to fathom that we love them so much, that we need to accept their absence to be at peace with ourselves once more?

How do we arise from a savage murder and how many days will it take to cure us? How do we comprehend death? Should we choose to tolerate death in return for a gift in the future? My acceptance is that one day I will have to die and will again meet my son. In the meantime, it is hard to think that he is not with me and not to know if he is safe or not.

I miss my son terribly; it has created a hole in our family and a big one in my heart. How long will it take for my broken heart to heal? Honestly, I will never be healed.

However, gradually you can begin to find some solace. These situations, such as a murder, are supposed to be dealt with through the legal system, but for us it is not necessarily the right system. Real justice would be to have our loved ones back. Acceptance then becomes another process that we experience. But for me, there is no final stage. There is no end, no closure yet. Those attackers are still out there; I cannot conceive of this injustice anymore. If there is real justice, then it will be in the beyond. This is what I truly believe. As I progressed forward from this time in my life, I hoped that life would take care of me and bring everything back to order. This reflection became my reality, fighting against the fear of staying paralyzed in the emotional spectrum of death.

For parents who have not lost a child, they may not completely understand the complexities of our loss. In regard to a child that has been murdered, denial and shock have a deeper level. This crisis was unanticipated, inconceivable and beyond belief.

In order to move forward, I had to reason that I could no longer be locked up tirelessly in the circle of pain, otherwise I would be there for the rest of my life. But this doesn't mean I cannot dream about him from time to time. In my mind, I would hold him between my arms, press him with my hand and on my chest, kiss his cheeks with a sense of pain, with an equally smug smile, my heart still wallowing in the indefinite. I closed my eyes a few moments and inhaled a long breath, remembering his smell.

My sufferance seemed longer for Michael than from other deaths I have encountered. I tried to find common sense out of his horrifying murder and understand why another human took away his innocent life. To me, it still remains incomprehensible to this day.

This random destructive action, executed by another person(s) remains dreadful, especially since the perpetrator(s) are still unknown. It comes as a shock, takes hold instantly and leaves you, your family, your friends surrounded and totally bewildered. It is hard to find peace. Such events cause unresolved conflicts and unsolved grief as the murderers are somewhere out there walking free, possibly laughing at you. Damn them... their smugness... their arrogance.

It feels like the anger is never going to end, it feels like it's deeper than other losses. I often try to find constructive ways to stop letting my anger out. But at the same time, I also *have* permission to let myself be angry. This often scares me, but I manage to keep it in perspective—how I am lucky to still have my other kids, my partner, friends and extended family.

I guess I have to look for forgiveness on my own time, at ease, and at my own pace. Forgiveness has to come from within, from the heart and soul.

Some days I wish people could know about my pain that still remains, possibly sharing it, to lighten the load. But they don't. How can they? Every grief is unique just like you are unique, just like a fingerprint is unique. I'm not sure yet how much I want to get involved in my son's murder case or even if I want to face it. Do I want to reopen the wounds?

I always refer to my organization, AFPAD. One of the members had her son killed beside her in bed when he was four years old. The assailant was her boyfriend; he was jealous of her little one so after a night out he entered the house, went to the bedroom and saw that he was sleeping with her and decided to kill him. That mother will never be the same, maybe she is ill, but that nightmare haunts her daily.

In the time since his death, I have helped myself heal by ceasing to feel everything they had done to him. Yes, my body was aching as if I had endured the same injuries as Michael. I am sure that those physical symptoms are directly caused by the mental distress. I now realize that those symptoms were caused by psychological phenomena referred to as somatization.

Maybe I made myself so miserable and so guilty that I provoke my body to become sick, leaving me with a scar in the place of his fatal wound, the blade that pierced his chest. I guess he just wanted to leave me with a tribute to him. I still ask myself: Was I the one who made myself ill, by thinking of his last moments and imagining that murder? I still cannot answer this question.

One thing I can tell you is that my body has felt every moment of that irreparable night. That scar, which I was so afraid would take away my femininity, has instead made me realize how precious life can be.

I was scared of the guilt of being happy again. I felt that my guilt would be more painful than continued suffering. But what I learned was: You can accept that the things that hurt us can teach us, can strengthen us. Possibly, to a certain degree, people who do not suffer can never truly know who their true inner selves are. We cannot be transformed without suffering because God is the sculptor of the marble of our stone.

Reminiscence

Chapter 18

Through many early mornings.
I saw his pains that were held in me.
His game of life was hard to play.
Here I am, saying hello to darkness again.
My old friend, I've come to talk with you again.
Softly creeping and dying while I was sleeping.
The vision that was planted in my brain still remains.
My restless dreams of the cold and damp puddle.
My eyes are stabbed by the glint of a flashing light.
A light that splits the night and touches that sound of silence again.
In the naked light I saw his decayed body.
People could be talking without speaking, hearing without listening.
Sharing his screaming melodies that their ears never heard.

If you are ready to change your life and your habits, you can do it. The day you are ready to let go, the moment you remove all your personal blocks, you will be on your way to your success. I created and established a list of my blocks. I had to accept Michael's suffering and stop deliberating on the murderers, this was my most significant block. At first, I did not accept that Michael never took the time to tell me that he was in danger or had bad relationships.

The concept of removing your personal blocks is paramount to your success. For a mother who loves her child so much it is the biggest milestone, since she may believe letting go is the same as ending her love for her deceased child. This is far from the truth, but it is the hardest thing to do, since we have let go a part of ourselves and we all think it's too much.

We should ask ourselves: How do I let go of my child? I love him so much. Love isn't possessiveness. Yes, you heard me: Love cannot be forever. Love is free, just like death and life, it comes and goes anytime. It exists everywhere, in every city, every country, every continent, it is everywhere and can happen anytime. Love is not chosen. Sometimes you have no idea why you loved somebody so much. The way you love your partner, children, and family does not belong to you, it comes and goes with life and death. There is nobody on this planet that loves another person in quite the same way. Love is free. Love is unique to all of us.

Even if you love someone solidly, for so long, and you never received anything in return, it doesn't belong to you. Love doesn't own you. So, by letting go you just let love move through you and through others. Yes, the love for the dead person is always present because that is the way love is. It is unconditional whether you know it or not, accept it or not. Love is sensational when it happens, but so painful when it is gone. There is no deficiency of love, we absolutely construct that blessing. We can create and offer as much as we want but we can't expect anything in return. Love is unconditional, especially for our children. There is no greater love, there is no measure, and so no way we can say how deep our love is.

I cannot say I love one child more than another. We set ourselves and our spirit in a mindset that we will be always loving them. I believe when you face death or a disappearance you simply have to realize that love will eventually drift away and you have to put your attention elsewhere or you are going to drift as well. We should concentrate our attention to our loved ones who are here on Earth and present, and stop paying so much attention to those in paradise, or wherever you call it.

Emotions are not always easy to control and the weirdest thing about them is that they never reflect reality. We are often disappointed by others, since we think that they do not feel the same way as we do, that they don't love us. Feeling a sense of loss is normal but in fact you did not lose anything as you never owned it. We don't own life, God does. Nobody has the power to make you feel better, only you do. You have to empower yourself with daily positive thinking, drown your emotions and navigate properly through your loss. Always be careful when you are dealing with emotions, they are volatile; make sure you do not sink by trying to rescue others, who arguably cannot be rescued. And above all else, try to avoid others who are angry, since their anger will ignite or rekindle your anger.

With so much drama in my life, I felt like I adopted the role of an actress in a movie of illusions. How many nights I thought I was in danger and that Hell's Angels would come and kill me? When I think about it now, it was none of those, nothing was reflecting reality. I should have known that to overcome Michael's death I needed to control my emotions and acknowledge that I was no better or worse than everyone else who had a similar loss.

If ever you encounter a horrific event, you should make the extra effort to always remember that life is a gift; it is a daily present, wrapped with a lovely bow with multiples stunning colours. Presents come in many sizes and many packages, as does life. So, take the position and trust that life is enjoyable, simple and on your side. Even if many times it took you in the wrong direction, always think that it took you on the road that is good for you, and that you were able to cross every crazy obstacle. You did it yourself, for you, and it was not in the way that others expected.

Letting go of another person is not easy. It is not like letting go of a car or a possession or anything else, it is letting go of a part of you. At first, the memories we retain of our loved ones may arguably hold us back, in the sense that we refuse to accept that our lovely togetherness is eternally gone. We find it tough sharing moments in the present, since we would prefer to resurrect the past; to adore every second, minute and day we have enjoyed with them. We just want to experience once again their touch, their hugs and their infectious grin. We fear letting go of our love once and for all, that everything we treasured in our shared past will no longer exist. The memories that used to bring us so much love, happiness and life now only bring misery. We clearly grip onto the past; it is so difficult to keep them active in our heads; we convince ourselves that happiness is gone, that it went with them to the grave, and we cannot find solace anywhere. We are essentially relinquishing our past life experiences for a future that we want them so much to continue with us. Every year, at his birthday, I will always make a cake. I now have another birthday to celebrate with him of course, my step-daughter's, and I will always ask myself what would it look like if they were blowing out the candles together. In my opinion, we have to envisage our dreams and stop thinking that we would have been better with them, causing us to overlook or forget about the others who are still alive.

I would argue that we unintentionally allow the deceased to be the keeper of our reveries, and therefore the guards of our lonely hearts. But how many days will we allow our hearts to remain tormented? The answer is: as few as possible. In my case, holding onto the anger towards Michael's murderers made me a slave to them. Trying to find them to prove what they did was wrong, without adequate justice, just pushed me further downward with more pain, hatred and a desire for revenge. It forced me to ask myself: Will it change the fact that he is dead? No! Will it affect the way I live the rest of my life? Yes!

In all honesty, if you were to ask me, "So you wish his murderers were dead?" I would answer, "Yes, I wish those assholes were dead!" But holding onto that sense of revenge, letting it control me, letting it consume me would not give me the freedom to enjoy life in the present. Again, I would be a slave to unconstructiveness and to those killers.

In my position, holding onto the chance that they would be found, with each fresh piece of information or with each new fragment of proof, only added to my disappointment and kept me in a state of misery. Since Michael's murder this has happened a number of times, from which, as new evidence became available, I was let down by my unfulfilled expectation of justice. So, what I forced myself to do was to let go of this anticipation to a certain degree. But I continue to believe that in the future, somehow, some special clue or particular person will come forward out of nowhere to help me find the truth.

An additional hurdle I had to overcome was that I couldn't stop thinking of what they had done to Michael. I had that image in my head of him dead laying in the ditch all the time. Even if every positive person, every family member or close friend was consoling me, I just couldn't get that picture out of my brain. Through the course of time, I have trained myself to compartmentalize that image. In other words, block it out. I still have the illustration in memory, but not in my mind.

As I mentioned at the beginning of this book, birth and death are the only two certainties we have in life. Spiritually, one could argue that we all end in the same place. But what we do between these two events is what really matters. Choosing to hold onto anger, mistrust, revenge will only prolong your suffering. What I did, and I encourage you to try, is to let go as much as possible of these feelings. In their place return to laughter, humour and light-heartedness. Laugh at yourself, laugh at and with others. This will not be easy. It sounds easy, but it is actually difficult and heavy. In itself, it seems a painful experience, and you want to dismiss this additional pain. But rest assured it will not diminish you as a person or parent. Yes, there will be pain, but why not kill the pain with pain? And of course, continue every day to ask yourself the same question: "How would my child like to see me now?" I'm sure that this will help you to feel lighter and less tragic about their death. Again, do not presume this task is easy, it will be a constant battle. But if I did it, so can you!

Michael has been dead for seven years and, in all honesty, I am still mourning. I sincerely agree that we never stop suffering completely. Part of my sorrow will always remain from the injustice and the thought that his killers are still free. If by chance these criminals are brought to justice, I will finally have peace of mind, and hopefully; greater confidence in the police

But the philosophy is that life is given as a finality of the knowledge of reality. Often it accesses the dimension of the untouchable world which is a necessary condition to access the truth, and therefore happiness. So, to distinguish the illusion of reality where we will discover its origin. We must reside in the recognition of our ignorance, motivation that can provide us with the motive for the search for truth. And if the human, his instability of its mortal survival, we are grateful to the existence that the soul of death has created in him.

Breaking the Isolation and Loneliness

Chapter 19

The quick loss of Michael left me with a limited opportunity to pay tribute to him. Looking back now, I am able to see how many times I should have taken better steps to fully accept my anger, commemorate his death and celebrate his accomplishments. But the anger I held towards Michael's killers, my ex-partners and my father were making me sink and lose my beliefs. It was harmful to my mind, body and spirit.

After his death, I was no longer the same; my life changed completely. The way I thought about people and about the world was as if everything was unpredictable and unstable. I just couldn't fit in that insane world anymore. Although I had never been a perfect mother, partner or person, I wanted to erase all my sins and live with admiration from my friends and family. I wanted to eliminate all the negative thoughts, acts and beliefs. I aimed for peace, serenity and love. I was longing for a bonded family I never had, and I wanted to be uniformly enjoyable to myself and to others. I was longing for an amazing transformation, but inside I was confused and hurting. They say that troubled situations pay off handsomely later if you really want them to, but I just wanted to be alone and isolated from reality. To deploy all your efforts, forget about your past and work for the life you really desire takes tremendous effort. Every day, I had to drag myself out of bed, drudge along with difficulty, and allow myself to even be a mini-me in the world. I really wanted myself to be happy, but I just couldn't believe in people anymore. I had to change my thinking completely and implement sanity and mental control in my daily routine.

To start with, I wrote my goals on a piece of paper and determined if they were really attainable. Then I endeavored to focus on these goals numerous times throughout the day, not compromising for anything else or letting myself drown in misery. Remember: *You are the only person who can change your life.*

It has taken me seven long years to complete that phase of my life; each day imagining a better existence. And yes, it took the murder of my son to challenge my inner happiness. And you can do this too! You just have to visualize it and find the tools to build it. I read a lot of books on positive thinking but the one that really helped me was: *Take Charge of Your Life* by William Glasser, MD (iUniverse, 2013). This book is about searching and the application of natural law to unify the thread of truth and enlightenment. Those of us who have lost a child struggle every day. Our emotions are volatile. And with each passing day, we may encounter crucial moments which change everything in our spirit. Those periods—or rather, situations, —are where our emotions have the opportunity to run wild. *It is vital that we control our emotions during these times*, otherwise we will aggravate our grief, confining ourselves further, preventing us from moving forward. Although, as the saying goes, "This is easier said than done", over time your tensions and anger will gradually decline until one day you will finally be released from your grief. Eventually, harmony will be restored within yourself, and between you, your friends and your loved ones. You will no longer be isolated if you apply the natural law of this universe that grows inside you and you accept the process of healing.

Even if my son's killers are still free and my pain persists, and some days I am on the verge of screaming out my frustrations, I have thought, or rather learned to focus my energy on patience, kindness and wisdom. When these situations arise, I write my frustrations on a piece of paper and burn them. Then I read passages from books with positive thoughts or self-help books that aid people in reaching their highest potential. This has become the most effective way to restore my mind and heart. Some people sometimes call me a miracle in life, or an example to others.

You may wonder, where does this ability come from? Or if having that wisdom comes easy? For some it is; for some it is not. We are all different and cannot compare ourselves to each other. We can ease each other with similar pain but can never feel exactly the same way, as we all harbour different bodies, minds and souls.

I would say that in the beginning, right after Michael was killed, I couldn't believe in anything. I wanted desperately to find the murderers. I wanted justice to be served. I wanted them to be put in jail. But this mindset was wrong. It just made things worse. I would constantly talk about the murderers instead of remembering the good times, displacing me from reality further, causing more disconnection from my family. Further, it was destroying all of my remaining positive feelings and ultimately allowing me to miss all the present moments with my family. In other words: This longing for closure, the endless wait for an unknown resolution led me to emptiness, sadness and further segregation. I isolated myself.

What I learned in the past seven years with respect to Michael's killers is that the more you search for them, the more you drown. To maintain your sanity, you must do the right thing—and this is to stop searching. To aid you with this task, stop listening to what everybody has to say. Focus and restore your good feelings, your inner flow, and associate yourself with the people you care about.

After your loss, it will be very hard to be in harmony with yourself, your friends, and your family, and to be in love again. You will have a hole in your heart and soul, which makes it difficult to talk to others, even with the most innovative grieving techniques and therapy. In order to change this, you have to realize that it is only *you* who has the power to change your life. What you have to force yourself to do, no matter how difficult it is, is start communicating again with others, even if you seem at a different level. Talk about your tragedy openly. Talk about your emotions and anger and ask them directly how they feel about theirs. Show them that their lives are good, their children are still here, and let them know their hopes and dreams are not shattered. It is normal to feel like you are the only one on the planet with a tragedy, but it will pass. Shift your focus slowly onto positive things, able yourself to the physical realm of life, laugh and love, even if it is for just five minutes a day.

As I mentioned in a previous chapter, it is important to journal during this time, to write down your feelings, thoughts and ideas *no matter how nonsensical they may seem.* Later on, go back and re-read your entries, possibly edit and rewrite them. Then compare the new to the old, to see how a few different words will completely change their intent or meaning. This change will be a reflection of how you have changed, hopefully in a positive way. Here are some entries that I made immediately after Michael was found, and today I reveal them for the first time:

> *I stock all that vague information, all that irritation and unfairness about his death. People try to help me, cheer me up or encourage me, but I think they don't want to help.*

But what I can say is that it won't help me. The important thing is to tell myself that they are family with bigger wounds than me.

If someone would ask me where to begin, I would not have an answer. I try my best at everything, but it seems I do not succeed. I thought that getting what I wanted, finding the killers, was what I needed. I felt so tired but I kept going. I couldn't even sleep because my brain wouldn't stop thinking. It was similar as when you're stuck in reverse gear. Then I would play a Coldplay song, Fix You, and sing it loud. So Loud: *…stuck in reverse / Lights will guide you home and ignite your bones…* I sang those words for months with all of my vocal cords.

Some days, I was so lost, lost in my sin, lost in my head, lost in my soul. Just to wonder where I had fallen or where had he fallen or where had we all fallen. How long had he been there? In that fuckin ditch. I wish someone could tell me the when, where and why.

But even if tears still stream down my face, even if I can't replace Michael, even if everything he had was thrown to waste, Yeah, because one day I was upset and I threw all his belongings in the garbage… done. What a stupid gesture as today I'll gladly aim a shirt that reminds me of my son. I remember also that his father was bothering me with his money collection and a couple valuable things he had. I hysterically threw everything on the porch and told him to keep it. I was not ready to do a triage of his things. How selfish is that when I am the one who had the shitty work to go to his apartment and clean everything. How could he ask me that when my son was not even buried? I was so mad, frantic and wrathful. I still hope that I would have been the light to guide him home and my love would ignite all his broken bones and sew his bloody wounds. I wish I was there that night, I would try to heal him.

Many days, months and years have passed, my body, spirit and soul are still lost, lost in that incomprehensive violence and unfairness. I pray to Michael high up and above. Once again, I am too involved to let go. What is the worth of our justice and the promise, that they will learn from all our mistakes? But how will I find what is near from the truth or far from the lies?

So many questions but no answers. But if I put a greater intensity of my visualities and feelings to a positive goal I will be drawn to the physical realm.

I now know that I'm not alone. Somehow, I'll find my way through that system and it will lead me to the trial. I hope my sun (my son) shall start rising again on those beautiful mornings when I am lying in my bed and feel the warmth of it on my skin. Michael had the habit to love the sun on his skin and lay everywhere in the house on the floor where the sun was penetrating through the windows. Today, my prevalent desire for my heart and to have peace of mind from those people not only he murders but the one who judged me. I know profoundly that there is probably no end and living is just an example that there is no guarantee of a possible in a human lifetime. Life starts and ends. But the end of our suffering is what we decide to with it. Mine is almost gone. My thought is that the way to extinguish desire of revenge, which causes suffering, *is to liberate oneself from the attachment.*

Today, it is July 2018, I've looked through Michael's belongings (the only one remaining is the black bag that they give you after the funeral ceremonial) almost seven years have passed. I reopened his trifling dark kitbag in the hope of coming across some information, clues or something to help me understand. Once again, I propel my mind in this insanity and wish that the investigators had hints. I would allow me to be free from that feeling.

Rather than hanging on to this thought I started putting my trust in words and actions, believing in the present in all the ways which allows me to relate to faith, love, hope, joy, and obedience to perfection. I self-master myself with love and secretly alter my prayers.

Somehow, I find that Michael is here with me, his brothers, sisters and friends. I scrutinize all the perfection he has done around him. I am now attuned to receive all the blessings that the universe sends me. There is only one world that we all come from and lets all dream of is that all people will melt into one, one day and that our deceased will be there, just holding our hand.

Astonishingly, on one particular day I found that I suffered from a lack of concentration. I just couldn't get focused anymore. I was dumbfounded; I just couldn't figure it out. So, I decided to take some time for myself; go for a walk to clear my mind. With no set destination in mind, I just walked, admiring the sky: azure blue with no clouds. I could hear the sound of the leaves in my ears like a harmony. I thought out loud, "where are you? What happened? I am getting trapped again in my horrible thoughts?"

When this happened to me, I realized that I had temporarily regressed back to some of my confusion, disorientation and isolation. This had happened to me many times before, after which I slowly recovered my mindset. But what I learned from this experience was the discovery that regression back to anger, depression, grieving and isolation could happen at any time. Of course, why not, I'm only human. The take-home message was that I would have to be cognizant of this regression for the rest of my life. And if it were to reappear, I would have to manage it using the methods I described earlier—talking to my spouse, my family, my in-laws. Not soon after, my focus shifted back to reality, permitting me to continue with writing and planning my future projects.

Another helpful way to help end your isolation is to find others who, like you, have had a similar loss. As I mentioned in a previous chapter, AFPAD has been an invaluable resource for me. This organization has aided me in so many ways. Besides teaching me that I was not alone in my suffering, one of the most important things that they showed me was that many other families have experienced bigger traumas, losses, than me. Like, the recent case where the mother of a two-year-old girl was charged with second-degree murder and committing an indignity to the dead body of her toddler. Her own baby. How sick is that? The mother appeared in provincial court dressed in a plaid shirt and wearing handcuffs. She was there to face charges in connection with the death of a child; she couldn't even acknowledge that it was her baby, as she's not even sure she remembers the facts. She seemed so cold. The child was only twenty-four months old.

The proceedings lasted less than two minutes. The woman looked out briefly at the packed courtroom before lowering her gaze to the ground. The toddler's body was found in a garbage bin at a suburban home. Police said the little girl had been stabbed to death. The woman was already in custody after being charged with breaching probation, obstructing the work of a police officer and mischief.

The Crown had six weeks to go through the evidence, gather some information and then present it to a judge. How long is that, though, for the life of a little child? Why is there so much suffering out there? But what of her parents? Not only have they lost their granddaughter, they also have to go through their daughter's unbelievable and atrocious trial—their daughter is now a murderer. How does a family heal from this? So many emotions must be floating around in their heads.

I think that the final verdict will be a second-degree murder charge, I think her actions speak for themselves. But I ask, What of the remaining family members? The parents are not even recognized as victims. The daughter will remain behind bars until her next court appearance, then probably plead insanity and be put on some type of therapy and drag things out for her next court appearance, and so on and so on. How many years do you think the victims have to wait until justice is served in the law courts? What can victims do to get better, faster court decisions? So, as you can see, there are families in worse predicaments. Hopefully, this helps to pull you back to reality, to keep your grounded!

Coping with grief and injustice is undoubtedly a daunting task. There are a few mental health professionals able to accurately diagnose and provide appropriate help for us. Those who decide to see a psychiatrist must choose one who specializes in mourning and grieving. Above all things, they will show you how to allow yourself to cry, to talk about your loss and accept your pain and emotions.

Frequently, many families remain without care, and with unanswered questions. They may also have to fight against a war of judgements. Without the judges, there are no labels to identify those who oppress our vendetta. That means that we mostly remain and survive without care. We are most likely trying to avenge death by ourselves. I believe that societal validation is simply scaled by insensitive people. In fact, they identify you as a bad parent and aim all the accusations against you. It is tricky, as you are in a crisis state of mind and thereby cannot defer to anyone, as you are scared to be judged. People for a while translated Michael's disappearance into a suicide or revenge over my brother. Even if there has been confirmation by the police that this was not related, people are still hooked on that version of gossip. Because of this I was isolating myself; I was ashamed of what my brother did, and that Michael could have ended his life. I had to break that isolation and start telling people that this was false. And even if Michael would have taken his own life, his actions were *not* a reflection on me.

For days, I refused to look at anything that was a grave. I was reminded that my name was not written on his tombstone. Even if many believe that it does not matter, I thought at first that seeing my son in the ground without my name robbed me of my inheritance of his soul. I remember going to Michael's grave on the first anniversary of his death. I remember removing dead leaves from his plot, leaf by leaf. My first instinct was to refuse to touch his tombstone. I was upset and heartbroken not seeing my name beside his. Then with both hands I threw the leaves in the air, as if we were playing together. Later, I asked myself, does it really matter? The conclusion I finally came to: Of course not!

Today, it is 10 August 2018, around 3 A.M. when everyone sleeps. The wind is calm, the magnificent sky of Calgary is full of stars. Once again, the silence of the night has turned into a nightmare. Out of the blue: A violent picture in my head, unleashed dogs are raging in the darkness of the night, looking for traces. Almost seven years and I am trying to remember: Everything took place in his apartment adjacent to the Riviere Chaudière on the 1st avenue St-Georges de Beauce. That night of 15 September 2011, when people decided his life was over. They chose to change my life, past, present and future by taking the life of my son Michael who was twenty-two years old, ruthlessly tearing my heart out with two hands, my flesh and my blood, a stab in his heart and in mine once again. I hope that time could stop, just like breathing, life or our smiles. I wish I could not see anymore, that I could stop the tears and the great pain that invades me even today.

My beliefs about our world have collapsed, but I still believe that there is goodness out there in the universe somewhere. We owe the universe all that is good in us, everything that rewards us in life. The most precious treasure is having the ability to put your suffering behind you. We are never protected from suffering, when we love someone else. No smile erases what pain is on a face, for those are not wrinkles, the look is the same. A person who has suffered has not necessarily aged, but transformed on a deeper level. For the brave who are suffering, it is like death is an all-encompassing occupation. And, during this time, it is important to acknowledge that your mental suffering may manifest itself with physical symptoms. Such symptoms are not imaginary, but real.

As part of my grieving process, and as a means of expanding upon my communication with others, I started talking privately to Michael as if he was alive. I told him every day to be grateful that at least they had found him, and that I would not be looking for his body anymore. I told him that I had started to forgive those people, the killers who had no remorse or guilt, those people who left him like a dog in a field. Even dogs that are found in a field do not suffer as much as my son had! This actually helped me to a significant degree, since it reaffirmed that I was trying to live my life in the same manner as before he was murdered. These everyday conversations, albeit brief, were accompanied by the crucial question: How would he like to see me now?

Many parents go through the departure of their child without finding the body or the murderers. This is the most heart-wrenching aspect of all. Not only is there the plight of relatives, friends, family and themselves, they have to deal with that anxiety and worry over the fate of the missing body.

Even if my time not knowing what happened to him had been for a short period, the two months felt like three years. Trying to cope with uncertainty about the fate of your missing child is the worst kind of grief. The emotional repercussions last long after and never really go away entirely.

From Michael's death I remain with pain and continue to manage my mental anguish. This anguish was sometimes accompanied by a wide array of symptoms, including isolated physical pain and illness. Anguish will often manifest in a form of anxiety and restlessness. It was not uncommon for me to wake up in the middle of the night in a pool of sweat. On other occasions, I would have large muscle cramps in my back and shoulders, and sometimes even chest pains. Those anxiety attacks could last hours and included widespread aches and pains including headaches and muscular tension.

You become driven by the anxiety, depression and all the other mental nuances imaginable. It is very important that you know and realize that those symptoms are not your imagination and they subside with time. Those are very real and can worsen your distress if you do not understand or have an awareness of the intimate connection between your physical and mental wellness.

So, by being aware and asking myself, "How would my son like to see me?" together with focusing on positive things and seeking out my inner self, I realized that all those tears were *not* necessary anymore. I had to learn how to *forgive* and that was the biggest step in my path to healing. Forgiveness is crucial. After a year of driving past the place where Michael had been found, I decided to take a detour and drive my car to the scene. My heart was racing, squeezing, but I had to do it. I had to feel his last breath. It was a bright day during fall, my favourite season. The sun was so warm and the sky so blue. I managed to drive all the way up until I passed the track where he had been found. A couple of minutes later, a couple arrived. It was the man who had found Michael. He was just going for a walk with his wife.

They looked at me and asked if I was the mom. I said, "Yes, and you are?" "We are the owners." We had a nice talk. Those people had nothing but kindness in their faces. They approached me and patted me on each shoulder. For ten minutes we didn't say a word. They knew that I was praying or imploring God. I wanted a miracle to happen.

Then the man told me purely and simply how he found my son. His words were calm and very deep. He described everything like it was yesterday.

Acceptance of Death

Chapter 20

How do you accept losing a child? I have never been a fanatic about fake smiles; when I am sad, I am sad, I do not pretend, and I am not afraid to show my emotions. After they found Michael, I began to feel angry. I had to return to work quickly and the downfall, unfairness and hate all began sinking in. I have always been a firm believer that people have the strength and faith to accept hardship in life, but after his death I was not so sure.

Who can you have faith in? I have wrestled with this question for many years now. Even if you try to ask this question of as many people as possible, or try to answer it the best you can, there simply is no real answer.

How often had I been disappointed in his investigation? I got swept up in each new story to the point of feeling euphoric, only to see my dreams tumbling down a few weeks or months later when the evidence went sour. Sometimes I wish for the early days when I thought he was still alive, so I could stop mourning his loss and avoid the tension that was created between myself and the people around me.

The disappearance and death of a child spares no aspect of your existence. Everything is overthrown and we even lose part of our own identity. It's like a huge storm that brings everything down, and in the after-math it is a huge task to rebuild our houses. Rebuilding is not an easy task, but we *can* do it. It's like the key of a piano when we learn our first notes. Sometimes we are born with the incredible talent for music while others work very hard to learn it. I had to deal with several notes that are still bitter in my mouth because the songs I had to sing became a sort of poison. There are no good or bad ways to accept a death or the disappearance of one's child. We just have to find a means to live with it. There are also no good or bad ways of living after someone finds your loved one's body mowed down by bastards.

We learn quietly through the years to manage our immense pain and our intense anger, even if it haunts us daily and even if in the depths of our soul, we want to erase the storm that slowly transforms itself, like the marvelous grains of the sand at the bottom of a beautiful blue sea illuminated by the majestic rays of sun, which, for just a moment, shimmers with the portrait of our child. Unfortunately for me, the storm passed and it destroyed everything in its path without giving me time to pull out a last memory.

There comes a time in life when it seems as if you are doing everything to please other people. It could be for your kids, your boss, your spouse or your parents. You just feel as though you have taken a back seat to everything and everybody around you. This becomes especially apparent after death; every passage of your life is affected and every area of your body is hurting. Essentially, you forget yourself and you start fading. This feeling of emptiness, or mere day-to-day existence, can last a very long time.

But I want to share with you something that is incredibly important: These feelings will eventually pass. When you start breaking away from death and that pattern and start pushing forward, you discover yourself again. You discover unimaginable strengths that you never had, and an inner glow. You finally realize that it is time to love yourself, your family, your friends and life once again. You start seeing everything change, you start seeing yourself in a new light, and you start seeing an abundance of love, laughs and joy in your life.

Personally, I would argue that most of my life has been built on misery. But I always believed that there was something good out there. Over the last couple of years, I have worked very hard on managing the emotions that losing Michael had created in my heart. It has been the most painful thing. Only God and parents of murdered children know what we have been through. I have strived so many times to keep going. The question I kept asking myself again and again and again was: How would Michael like to see me now? That is the question that kept me focused, and still does. I knew that my son would want to see me shine, be successful and, above all else, be happy. This notion formed the basis for my healing process, and ultimately, acceptance of his death.

But if true happiness is your goal, if you yearn for happiness and freedom from the emotional turmoil caused by death, you cannot obtain this state of mind without first accepting death. As I mentioned in the beginning of this book, life has two certainties: life and death. Put another way, death is a part of life; you cannot have the two separately, since they are intimately related.

Even if our grief can diminish our spiritual strength, we can still define it. The experiences of having someone in hospital whose health declines can cause us to question our spirituality. It can seem too unfair that someone we love so much is dying. It's hard to see them suffer through pain and disease, but at least there is closure.

My closure has not happened yet. I find this deluding. When Michael died, I had no idea why and how long he had suffered. As a result, many scenarios went through my head. It is only normal that I might question myself about the benevolence of the world or of a higher power. Should we have to hold onto our beliefs? This is the ultimate question for us, the believers of faith and God, even if there are still so many questions that remain unanswered. I still ask myself where is God when we need him? And why this is happening to me? Why have I become the master of pain and suffering?

Is it because of our choice to reject happiness? Or live in a world that has fallen apart, full of pain, despair and all kinds of sickness? With all that confusion you begin to realize that mental anguish affects you on so many levels; you become a stranger to your own body and mind. But I would argue that this is not humanity's purpose. Are we really meant to live without pain, sadness or trouble?

Previously, I asked: How can we sacrifice our own child to pay the price of our sins? Isn't that the wrong price? It is so hard to imagine that we have to force ourselves to let someone we love go. How do we rise from death? And how many days does it take to cure? How can we accept the power of death over the human spirit? More importantly, from his death, is there anything that I can philosophically reward myself with? I suppose from this point of view, and as part of my acceptance, I hold that one day after my death I will have the opportunity to meet my son again. But in the present, it is hard to think that he is not with me and not know whether he is safe.

Can we fully recover from the death of our child?

From my perspective and experience, no, we do not recover. As any parent will tell you, we just learn to live with it, no matter how painful. It is the hardest pain to live with, because it is not natural for a parent to lose a child—it breaks the circle of life. Simply put: A child should not die before his parents.

Is death as a consequence of an act of violence more difficult to overcome? I would argue yes, it is. What complicates acceptance is barbarism. When death is not "beautiful" or "peaceful," it's even harder to fathom. We need to see the body to say goodbye, yet some parents will not have the opportunity; they are restricted by circumstance or the law. They will imagine the worst things. We need to know how they died. We want to trace their last moments alive. We will seek officials; we will blame this or that group. It's hard to be totally resilient; some of the mother's own flesh is, after all, dead.

What are the stages for families who have lost a child?

First, there is shock at the announcement. Then parents will go through powerful denial mechanisms, so long as the body is not found or identified (some are damaged), they will be convinced that the child is still alive. This may prevent them from progressing to the next stage of grieving: anger. Most of us are conditioned to suppress our anger, but this is a necessary step in grieving. It gives structure to the feelings of nothingness caused by your loss. We may become angered at family, friends, strangers and ultimately for the deceased. The latter arises, since we feel abandoned by them. We convince ourselves that the loved one selfishly left us alone. During this time, it is important to understand that this developed anger is really a true reflection of our intensity of love for our deceased.

Next, individuals will go into a state of bargaining, where they question themselves with, "What if I had done this instead?" This represents a period of a loss of confidence in ourselves and an introspective search for our faults. Generally speaking, people will bargain for an end to their pain, against future conduct or actions. Following this, people will enter into a depressive state. After transitioning into depression, these symptoms may be exacerbated by flashes of memories, as parents realize their child will not be back. The absence of the child will be loudest at family gatherings, be it for Sunday family dinners, at Christmas, during birthdays, Mother's Day, Father's Day. It is important to realize that depression is not a sign of mental illness, but rather a response to our enormous loss. Finally, we enter into acceptance. With this phase, we readjust our lives to deal with the new reality that our loved ones are physically gone. We come to the understanding that we cannot bring them back, but we can make a difference to ourselves and others around us. From here on, we start to rebuild our lives, rekindle connections with friends and invest our time in the lives of our living family members. Put another way: We detach ourselves from the deceased and regain a taste for life, even if a slight prohibition to enjoy life still weighs on us.

The look of others weighs a lot on our psyche. They say that only the wise man who continues to live is capable of resilience. Fathers and mothers bear great guilt on themselves. A parent is there to protect their child, even when he is grown up. He will say to himself, "But I did not feel this coming. He called me an hour before saying this or that." Again, as part of our bargaining stage, we the parents convince ourselves that we could have saved our child. This is erroneous, but often considered. This will do nothing but continue to propagate your self-deception and self-punishment.

I would say that all mourning parents want to search, in their own way, for the people who saw their child prior to the murder. We want to know the exact circumstances of their death. Even if this feels like a positive step toward finding peace, it is actually destructive. In my case, on some days I would find an explanation, and then on other days I would be immediately swept up by another version. It feels like being the deceived husband who wants to know all the details of his wife's adventures. Yet that will not solve the problem. Relating back to murder, the child will still be dead.

I have to admit that my mind and spirit are still not fully clear. Some days are worse then others. Maybe I should take antidepressants for it, but would that be appropriate? No, I do not think it would be. If I now underwent another reassessment from a physician, they would reinforce that my depression was a result of Michael's murder. I also think that they would tell me that it would be unhealthy for me to continue focusing on

Michael's unsolved murder. To the contrary, I think they would tell me that I have to remember him as he was—in a baby picture, or during my last visit to his apartment. Now his photo is in the same place as all the other photos of my family. I simply continue my life with him in my head and my heart. Life goes on; the Earth continues to turn.

Shortly after Michael passed away there was no way for me to resume my daily routine at work. I had too much respect for my clients to not give them my usual work ethic and service quality. I had no confidence in life; I was afraid of making errors and afraid to hurt my boss. So, I took a leave of absence. One thing I did do; which in hindsight was great, was to volunteer for local charities. I think volunteering gave me an outlet to continue working is some fashion. I think it gave me purpose. We all need purpose! It allowed me to prove to myself that I was still fit to help. I stayed in contact with my police colleagues, but the wait for the conviction of Michael's murderers was still ongoing. At that time, things appeared to be reasonably okay.

As I mentioned previously, there are organizations and specialized therapists to help us. But I didn't choose that path. I found this to be time-consuming and of little value. It was all about contacting them for medical follow-ups every month, psychological follow-ups every week, police follow-ups for each installment of legal proceedings. In other words: A lot of investment with no results.

Looking back, I now realize that through this time, and over the past seven years, I should have continued with these appointments. They would have helped me hasten my healing, psychological reparation, understanding and emotional readjustment to my life going forward. If you are grieving, I encourage you to take advantage of these opportunities. It will surely help you reclaim your life and strengthen you as you move forward.

Frankly speaking, my lingering, albeit diminished pain is internal and only my spouse knows of it. I talk to myself, I breathe, I pray. I think I'm going to die, but I don't, and today I am here, with you and all the other people who have suffered similar losses. I know there will always be a chair with nobody sitting in it around the dinner table, and a picture of him on his twenty-second birthday to insert into our family portraits. The impacts?

Mine? Yours? The impacts are infinite. Sometimes I feel as though I hate the world and everybody in it. But I recognize these as the residual impacts still residing in me. I have learned to manage and control them, preventing them from overrunning and consuming me.

There will always be less noise, and less food to prepare during festivities. There will always be a son missing. Society and one family are both without a person who believed that everyone has goodness and hidden potential, a person who wanted to help others to be better. I must see other skies, other clouds with other suns. My little grandchildren and my children are part of it now. I have to laugh for them; I have to sing for them. I have to put on a mask for them and for everybody. I have to give my daughter Kelly-Ann and my spouse all the love they rightly deserve. Just because it will never be the same again for me doesn't mean it has to be the same for them.

One of my life dreams has collapsed; the loss of my child in a way destroyed, sabotaged one of my deepest convictions: preventing violence towards the weak ones.

Unfortunately, we have to believe love was not enough. Not enough to discover that this has forfeited my financial, marital, family status quo. It goes without saying: "Destabilization" is the term that summarizes my life and still does after seven years.

My goals now are simple: to make myself useful to society and to my family and use my pain as an ally. My worst mistake would be to try to minimize or eliminate that pain, because it is now part of me. I have to tame it daily. Like a wicked nemesis, she will continue on with me. Even if I do not accept it, she accompanies me everywhere, every minute of the day. That's my feeling in just a few words. I could write pages and pages again. But I made it brief: The murderers of my son are still out there. I am not one hundred percent sure it wasn't an act of revenge; my emotional stability is still shaken. I hope you can see my plight. There have been so many souls affected by this—his soul, my soul, your soul. The young adults out there who know that they took his life away and choose not to repent their sins. To the killers, I pose: Where is your heart, your reason, your judgment?

But even today, I have to go back to my other children with the burden of judgment and gossip of society. It still lingers. I sometimes try to over-invest in Michael's siblings and my grandchildren because he took up more time in my life than the others. I am happy, though, not to be like some parents who have fetishes over their child's possessions. Some keep things to keep the child present longer with souvenirs, pictures, smells, but I had none of this. I threw most of his belongings in the garbage. Although his little black bag has remained in my closet, intact for seven years. I'm sure it still smells of the perished bananas and the rancid smell of his apartment. How can we have a favourite child when we love them all so differently, but only one murdered child? Is it even worse?

Did the fact that his death was part of an ultra-publicized event change my grieving? No, it didn't. The day the cameras, microphones, social media left us alone, things changed. I hope that Michael will not feel forgotten or betrayed by the fact that there is nothing to say to any of those people.

What positive role can you and your entourage play? What can we, parents of murdered children do to get better? These are the two questions…

As mentioned earlier, we should make the conscious decision to see a psychologist or psychiatrist, one who specializes in grieving and bereavement. Possibly, we can contact the association AFPAD, or refer to a very good book regarding this issue. But as I stated before, there are no books to really help us completely. We must be careful not to force ourselves to do things to the extreme. If we do not want to go out, then we should stay home, but it is *not* good to stay isolated. We must accept suffering to a small degree. We must allow ourselves to cry, to talk and to accept pain and emotions. If we block the world, no one will be able to communicate with us. Keep a journal, write in it every day. Record your emotions, or whatever comes to your mind. I used to write poems each day. Poetry can be abstract, a loose assortment of thoughts, feelings, words. That is why I used poetry during my grieving period. It matched my mindset. Here are my favorite poems:

On our ancient threshold, you disappeared without warning.
I wish I could be the rain covering the lonely moors, the wind

that denudes the fragile trees that were surrounding the body of yours.

I wish I knew the difficulties that dwelled in your thoughts and made you make those choices, the difficulties that ran through your head, like a reptile, so your soul wouldn't get lost in the sweet madness.

I wish that the silence would speak and the earth would leave other people more attentive to them seeking and to us the crying moms, who agonize will heal all our broken hearts and have time to sympathize. I wish that the island that hosts false starts would float with integrity. And that one that has the answer would be cover in the asphalt of helpless love.

That the glade of that sad power will find the weapon that annihilates the past and present in which would hide his words: "I wish I could be the light that ignited your broken bones and knocks to the heart of the murder to make him fell my emotions." Beside despair, that my bare expectations of the heart, the heartbreaking temptation to find you, the fever that lights, the passion of a mother and your absence will be the twilight of reason to find your killers.

Now, I am withering in the unreal. I am the heartbreak of life. I am the excess in the carnal and to exile that spirit that the fire of hell has consumed. I have become this poor feather who writes these words in the wind of hope.

Imagining the Worst

Chapter 21

Some days, I feel like I am looking through a broken window. Under the influence of anger, I rummage through everything. I see in his eyes an influx of dew, vibrations of the heart, reflection of his thoughts, his mind is still in my soul and my broken heart reflects on the mirror of the pieces of the fragmented glass.

If at least he would have told me, "I'm leaving you now, you will not see me anymore," I would have been prepared for the shock. I told him so often, "Never leave without saying where you're going," and he always followed my advice. Today I am watching his ride. He crosses the track, it's already in the past. He leaves, abandoning everything behind him, he deserts without telling me where he departed, he spreads his wings through the magnificent blue sky where no one sees him.

Seven years and I still live in the hope that one day he will turn around and tell me why he left and where he went. But no, he's twirling away dressed in a big black cape and it impossible to glimpse his face. I would trade all my nights to find him, retrieve him from the foreign arms that would have discovered him alive. Deep in my soul, I finally distinguish that nobody crossed his path. This mother who stills revolves around sorrow tries to leave the deserted track.

Soon I will see that the storm will pass and I will understand that he will not come back. That the last key unlocked the injuries of the heart. Even if I open my heart to others, even if I am destined to love, I would love to see him again just a moment. I wish somebody could give me a moment with him…

If his life is now just a memory, then let me remember it with him. I wish our hearts could be like flowers and as fragile as all the hours I spent with him.

Let's hold to that memory and never let it end. If feelings are surrendered, let them surrender to him. Even if yesterday I was lonely, he only has to bring some tears to me to kiss away the sadness and the pain I feel. The impression of a warm summer day embraces my thoughts and I just want to fly around him. But today the sun is shining without him, but it still leaves warmth without bitterness.

So many times, I stopped myself from healing just by imagining everything they had done to him. For over one year my body was aching and my mind focused on negative thoughts. I made myself so miserable and so guilty that I crippled myself with an unnecessary fear. Physical symptoms were directly caused by my mental anguish and distress—I experienced somatization, hurting my own consciousness and body. Again, the scar that I have today on my breast is at the same place as the final jolt that took him away from me. That scar has the same dimension of the blade that pierced his chest. It is located on the same side and is the same length. How is it that we mothers can feel our child? Is it real or unreal? I knew he was suffering and could feel those blades pierce my soul. Some days I grafted my scar into his, and believed he wanted to leave me with a souvenir. Or did I just imagine that? Thinking about his last moments, visualizing the murder and how they killed him was the biggest thing to heal from and I don't think I will ever fully recover from it. But on the flipside, the wound it left made me realize how precious life is, changing it forever.

As I began to move forward, I decided that I was fortunate and blessed that the hunters had found my son. Right after Michael went missing, I had many dreams, or rather, premonitions, that he would be found face down in a ditch. Although they varied in different contexts, they all had the same theme. I believe that Michael was communicating hope to me, to find his body and to reassure me that he was now at peace. Repeating these dreams revealed life, death and grief, but were without the reference of time. I suppose events in your dreams are generalizations; i.e., they all come at any time and look all the same, but we should always be open to what our child is trying to convey to us in a dream.

For some reason, at that time I couldn't split up from his existence. I felt compelled to receive his calls and I fought with this pretty much every day for two years. It was so bizarre. I was so lost in love.

It was such an exhausting situation with nothing to gain except sorrow, pain and heartache. I think they call this dynamic projection. I projected a lot of my childhood, a lot of anger from the past and I got trapped when it was projected back at me.

Projection is what happens when you attribute your own emotions to somebody else. When all your life your parents have been in a fight, even if there was no physical contact between them, you get a dynamic that keeps you locked in a combative mode that provokes nothing other than anger, conflict and dissention. You subconsciously attribute your emotions to your kids, partner and events. It's like projecting a movie to a screen. These emotions are in you but it looks like it comes from the other person. It typically happens to most of the family members who have been raised in that environment.

Looking back, my projection was almost completely related to anger. Not anger from the loss of Michael, but anger from my past. I was angry that my father used to beat, abuse and enslave my mother. I was angry at my mother because she was scared to leave my dad. I was angry because sometimes she was not there for me, even though my dad beat her so much that she had to stay in hospital for days, even though it wasn't her fault. Later, I was angry that she left my dad and that I was not seeing him anymore. Then after that, I was angry because she had a new boyfriend and she would leave me for him.

I was angry at life in general. Life was so unfair. I was carrying that anger since I was a child, and subconsciously I probably didn't want to own my own feelings; I didn't want to live with them. So, I had to own more, realize that life is short and precious and that life and love exist, you just have to see it. I guess for many years I saw partners as angry and abusive even though I was the one secretly consumed by anger.

Relating back to the grieving process, you have the potential to make people suffer because of your anger, but unfortunately; you don't realize you doing it. It is as if you are wearing blinders. You have so much trouble seeing it in yourself. There were so many things I was angry about, and they were not easy to get away from. But today, with my newfound inner strength together with support from my older kids and my new partner who was raised in a loving and stable family, I can honestly say that I don't have that anger anymore. This is so important, it is your first big step in your movement forward.

Oddly enough, I suppose, I started a process of self-reflection. One could argue that this was a positive outcome of Michael's death. I started to analyze my fears, coming to the conclusion that my greatest fear: was the fear of death. I started looking back on my life of all the supposed fears I used to hold—the fear of not doing my job well, the fear of losing my job, the fear of not providing for my children, the fear of not being in a relationship, the fear of not being a good spouse. But all these were put into perspective by Michael's disappearance. All those fears that I thought were so paramount were really miniscule in comparison to the fear of death. I would say that this reflection gave me a new outlook on life, giving me the ability to face all those small fears more easily.

Facing one fear is actually the starting point for facing all of the others. For most of us, we are afraid of failing because we are not up to it. We are afraid of losing our friends, of being abandoned, of being rejected because we are not up to it. We are afraid of intimacy for the same reason: we could be rejected because we are not up to it. Even the fear of success is based on the concern that we are not up to it. The fear of losing what we have prevents us from having success.

Being afraid is natural. But letting it keep you from chasing your dreams is a tragedy. I would say that once you surpass your fear and premonitions— you will start to live life to its fullest.

With this in mind, we should be aware that in adulthood, we become parents ourselves and we fear losing our children. This is indeed the response of online searches that come back most often when asked about parents' fears. Because becoming a parent also means realizing how precious and precarious life is. We realize how our parents have suffered to raise us and give us the necessities of life. How can we, as parents, imagine that those of a criminal nature are so difficult to quantify? But when you are confronted with their disappearance and the uncertainty of finding them, it is difficult to quantify your fear.

This is a terrible paradox! The more we settle in life, the more we become aware of all the risks that there are to life, and the closer we get to the three unthinkables, which are illness, aging and death. With all of these, we have no control and cannot do anything to prevent them, then the circle closes. Perhaps the fear of death is only the memory of the fear of being born?

Everyone has their personal story about fear, a connection that has been built from the most important episodes of our lives. This has been my case for over the past seven years. But I will not let the fear prevent me from even trying or daring to dream again.

In my thinking, we are the victims of others, which is worse. We cannot predict any of this and to be soothed; there is only one solution: Get rid of smaller fears, eliminate them, the gossips, one by one, and then go to the greater fear, the killers. I know this is not very attractive or doesn't make much sense, but it is the path that everyone is invited to follow to understand this chaos, which is so irrational. We need to ensure that society will put in place more sophisticated systems to make it safer for people, find the proper antibiotics for the illness, and nothing will make us feel better. And if people understand our feelings, the panic when our child who disappeared under criminal circumstances is missing and that this has nothing to do with the parents, if everybody would go through severe acute respiratory syndrome, we would be aware that not only do their own little personal fears count, but the big threats would reach people at least half as much.

It is easy to blame others for all that's gone wrong in your life. But it is also very hard to live with remorse and make people around you miserable. What happens in crucial moments can change everything for those who have been struggling with death. With time, you will develop a wisdom that helps melt away tensions, restoring harmony between you, your friends and your loved ones.

However, you may wonder if having that wisdom is simple. For some it is, for some, like me, it is not. So many days and nights I painfully forced myself to remember the events around Michael's death, dredging up the manuscript of this book. I wrote down page after page, then crumpled the paper and said that I'd never get there. Sometimes I could barely read what I had written, as tears were streaming down my face, let alone relate to the characters mentioned within the pages. After writing, emotionally drained, I would feel like a baby in a grown-up world. Nonetheless, writing this book means a lot to me, and so many times I wondered whether my motivation to write this book would have collapsed along with so much else. My fingers move over the keyboard very slowly and with uncertainty; I begin to jot down a bit of what I have been going through. I finally talked to a person from AFPAD and then I made a list of the families who have lost their children and realized that I am not alone. By being in contact with others suffering like me, I could not help but see my own humanity. I think seeing my humanity has aided me in moving forward after Michael's murder.

We think that in order to have peace we have to discover it, or earn it. We talk about it all the time. We talk to friends, family, colleagues; we are compelled to know, to hear, to find. We keep all the negative thoughts and feelings to ourselves, even if every day we put a smile on our face and pretend everything is okay. We avoid reality and think that peace is only a dream. But what we have not realized is that approach leads to more disconnection from our feelings and the sharing of great moments with the ones we love who are still in our lives. From what I have learned over the past seven years, this longing for closure, this dream of peace, this endless wait and the unknown leads us to more emptiness.

After murder, your heart is not able to communicate effectively. You try as hard as you can to yell that you're lost, but sometimes is seems as though nobody is there to hear you. You take stock in all that vague information, that irritation and unfairness about their death. You fuel yourself with only that drama, you think that you will never be able to have your inner peace. But then you realize that only you have the power to change your life. And for those to whom this realization happens, it seems too good to be true.

What has kept me positive is the knowledge that there are so many other families that have experienced bigger traumas then me.

If someone were to ask me where to begin healing or how to move forward, I honestly would not have the right answers. You just have to drudge through it all. Bear in mind, as you progress forward you will likely have roadblocks. You try your best at everything but it seems you don't succeed. When you feel so tired but you can't sleep because you mind is too active, at other times it will seem like you are stuck in reverse, then on other days you will be lost, lost in your head, even lost in your soul. But rest assured, with patience, you will overcome these blocks. And each time you do succeed, you will become a little stronger.

I know now that I'm not alone. Somehow, I will find my way through that system and it will lead me to the trial. I hope my sunshine (my son) shall start rising again on those beautiful mornings when I am lying in my bed with the warmth of it on my skin. Michael used to lie everywhere in the house on the floor where the sun was penetrating the windows.

My biggest desire is for my heart to be at peace from those people, and if they're asking me when, I'll say it all starts at the end of the suffering.

You know, I have looked through Michael's belongings. After almost seven years, I reopened the black bag in the hope of coming across some information or clues or something to help me understand. I wish that the investigators had clues. It would allow me to be free from that feeling of trust and rather learn to put my trust in God, who is believed to be present in ways which allow me to be related to in faith, love, hope, joy and obedience. It is secretly matched with love, and that talk alters my prayers. Somehow, I find that Michael is here with me, with his brothers, sisters and his friends. All are close by his side and speak to him every day. One day my season's wish will come true and all the seasons will begin with him. There is only one world that we all come from and the one I am dreaming of is that one world where you will just hold my hand and we're there somehow. We're all be going somewhere.

I think suffering is caused by an attachment or some kind of nonsense that we hold on to. It can be a positive outcome, a negative one or simply an avoidance of the truth. In order to offset external roadblocks, it is important for you to identify and address your internal roadblocks. Parents of murdered children often confuse ourselves, believing that letting go of our children is the same as letting go of our love for them. In my opinion this is a formidable roadblock, and a huge misunderstanding of the concept. Simply, we cannot let go of our love for our children. So many of you are therefore going to ask yourselves, "How do I let go of my child?" In my opinion we have little choice. It is now our new reality. But we will never, never, never end our love for them!

We allow that dead person to be the keeper of our dreams. How many days will our heart be injured for? That's how we become the slaves of those killers. We have to make sure we hang onto the proof and it requires us to hang onto false hope. It's as if by staying, we are trying to prove that we are indeed worthwhile of judgement, resentfulness and revenge. Because it is about seeing ourselves as separate from the rest of the world and somehow a special clue or person will come out of nowhere and help us find the truth. We can't let go, because that threatens our ego, our motherhood or our selfishness. Letting go of the murderers is like letting go of a part of yourself and placing it into the trash to diminish our consciousness.

Sometimes I felt like I was living in an illusion. I cannot remember how many times I had to deal with people dramatizing or asking me if I was in a movie of hallucinations. How many nights was I in danger? When I think about it, maybe nothing of this was reflecting reality but now I know that I did overcome it. I learned to control my emotions and to accept that I was not better or worse than everyone else who has had a similar loss.

During your grieving period, there is a lack of trust in everything and everyone around you. Oh my God! You don't even trust yourself after an event like this. Trusting life and people is a huge issue. But as you move forward, your trust in it will begin to normalize. Part of this process may be retarded by a betrayal or a troubled past. But eventually you will begin to realize or remember that life is beautiful, life is a gift every day—that's when you can make the choice to trust that life is good, simple and that life is on your side. Even if many times life brought you in the wrong direction, always think that it brought you on a road that is good for you and that you are able to cross. Let go, allow yourself to be truly happy and joyful. You just have to remind yourself that you had taken many different paths. Remember, we all end in the same city: Paradise City. Choosing to hold onto anger and not trust again means you are stagnant, stuck in suffering. The best way to help yourself is to let go of all of this!

My Unanswered Questions

Chapter 22

There is no doubt that unanswered questions make us suffer. However intense or devoid of meaning, answers are necessary, and are useful in the relief of the pain. If people could be conscious of all that enigma created by death, and how unhealthy and puzzling our minds become, they would give more importance to understanding our moods. Even if suffering became a great part of my existence, it made me understand that I had to suffer to be free to continue my life with my other children.

What allows us, as human beings, to survive psychologically, physically and mentally; to live on earth with all its pains, dramas and challenges, is to have a sense of accomplishment and a life of meaning. In every difficult moment I have lived, felt and experienced, it has given me the potential to open my eyes, my heart and my soul to more compassion, understanding and tolerance. Within and against the pleasures of the happiest people in the world, I would not exchange the evils I suffered, as now I have discovered a profound comfort and happiness in my life. With all of my suffering, I have been equally rewarded with happiness. I believe that within the highest attainment of suffering comes a paralysis of sensibility, but as soon as we provide kindness to others, our paralysis dissolves, we stop feeling sick, we stop suffering, and we discover the meaning of the statement "Giving *is* Receiving." I found that with my spouse, I now have more than I hoped for—I am now suffering less, because of our charity work in South America.

But if there are things that are not seen properly, they can only be seen with eyes that have cried. I learned that there are no bad people, there are only people who have not found other ways other than hurting others to manage their own suffering. When we are happy, do we want to look to others for stories?

I now feel that I am stronger than at anytime other time in my life. Anything bad which could have happened to me, has happened! All these things—sadness, misfortune, loss and suffering—are in front of my porch. I am in the house of happiness, and I am the only one who has found the key. The most enduring quality about humans is our ability to create, overcome, endure and transform. Love overcomes our suffering. Joy still arises when my little grandson is tired and cries with all his lungs, his mom easing his suffering by breastfeeding him.

In my experience, the worst part of suffering, was the thought that I could no longer love again. But that door had two keys: one called sorrow, the other called patience. Sorrow was the force that drove me into action and made me humble. But I realized I had no choice, I had to develop patience to endure it. When you realize that you have no choice but to endure it, you will develop patience or courage to tackle your own suffering. Just like me, you will find it is wonderful when you heal, when you turn suffering into compassion. When you obtain acceptance… ultimately moving onward and upward.

Some have a list (suffering) which is significantly bigger than mine. I cling to enlightenment and continue writing on my computer and gazing at the words; telling myself that, finally, I have moved on. Compared to others, I say to myself that in my bad luck… I was lucky.

To see someone, you love suffering is one of the worst feelings in the world. Wanting to get rid of all suffering means evading an essential part of human life, even if sometimes we think that they are super-human. If you could keep your heart marveling at all the daily miracles in your life, your pain would be considerably less than your joy. You would accept the seasons of your heart, as you have always accepted the seasons that pass over your fields, and you would watch with serenity, the "winters of your sorrows."

The deeper the grief which digs into your being, the more you will be able to create joy to calm your soul. It is only through suffering that the soul becomes stronger, adding to your success. For although this world is full of suffering, it is also full of victories. They say anything that does not kill us makes us stronger. And through the suffering, there is something that must be learned, something that can never be fully described: one can recover from suffering only if one feels it fully. But, the biggest suffering is to feel alone, without love, and abandoned by all. When this degree suffering falls on our lives, we must accept it with a smile, says Mother Teresa.

People with a criminal personality fail to learn from their previous mistakes, even if the consequences lead them to the justice system. Hence why these individuals engage in such activities repeatedly throughout their lives, as they are often very deceitful. Why is there repeated lying about the events and circumstances, uses of aliases or even conning others for personal profit or pleasure? I guess there will never be an answer for this. Why do they not deliver themselves to the police when they savagely slay someone? How can a human specimen live with a murder on his conscience?

In the state of this affair, the police deem that the murders tried to promote themselves to achieve a higher rank in the eyes of the Hell's Angels. They used Michael's murder to scare all the other little dealers. They used this to make a statement that others will suffer the same consequence as Michael if they choose to work for their competitors. In St-Georges, there are a couple of individuals who were trying to prove that they had control over pills and pot and were using young adults to "wash their dirty clothes" through enticement. The provincial police revealed that they had never seen so many people reporting to their office, lining up, saying that they knew who the murderers were, that these individuals were using my son's murder to scare others. They turned on their charm, and in order to mask their crime they made the victim guilty, just as simply as they outlined him, saying that he was the one who owed money to the Hell's Angels. Not only are they trying to exploit the system and make everybody lose their time, they are arrogant and even brag about it, thinking that they will never be caught.

Through irresponsible behaviour, such as persistent lying, manipulation and disrespect for others, they prefer passing the blame to others by concealing their tracks. I am convinced that the reason they do this is for their own personal gain. They kill with such ease and don't have empathy for us the families. They lack the ability to figuratively step into another person's shoes and understand their feelings. The mental state of others does not factor into their decisions or their actions. As a result, they often end up causing others, such as their friends, a great deal of pain. They are unable to reason why a person would be hurt by their actions. They don't feel bad for what they have done and will therefore likely repeat the behavior many times in the future.

Those individuals don't care about others as they don't have the same ability to control their impulses like most. When the average person thinks about doing something that would result in immediate satisfaction, they are able to restrain their urge. Simple things like stealing a simple purse does not apply to a vicious person. Because of their unconstrained and impulsive behaviours, those stealers of lives will only receive a lesser charge like a second- or third-degree murder.

I miss my son terribly. His horrible murder has created an enormous hole in my heart. How long will it take my broken heart to heal? Honestly, I do not think it ever will, even if gradually I have found some solace. I still want an answer to my question. Who killed him? I know someone knows something, somewhere.

For me, there is no final stage yet, nothing has ended and there is no end to my movie and to my suffering. Those who have lost a child due to another cause may not always completely understand the complexities of our loss. The denial and shock that Michael had been murdered consumed me at a deeper level. The crisis that was unanticipated, inconceivable and still remains beyond belief. I feel agony yet no closure. My spouse always asks me, "If you were to make a movie about this, how will you end it?" I answer, "I would simply tell people that there is no end." We have no idea who it was. We have a loose assortment of facts, and collected information from here and there, but we do not really know the truth, as nothing has been proven yet. I live in the spur of the moment, and hope every day that the phone will ring and they will provide me with the answer. But I have no idea when, who, how, why. In still feel as blind as a bat.

Some days I try to make sense of all of this. Murder is horrifying because another human took away an innocent life. It is incomprehensible that another person took him away from me, let alone it could be somebody that I know? It took a hold of me and my family instantly, leaving us totally bewildered. It makes it harder to find peace, since the murderers are somewhere out there, walking free.

My anger, although substantially diminished and under control, feels like it is never going to end. It feels like it is deeper than other losses. I often try to find a constructive way to let my anger out but, as explained by my psychologist; I *have* permission to let myself be angry. I guess I have to look for forgiveness on my own time, at my ease and at my own pace. Forgiveness has to come from within the heart and soul. Some days I wish others could know the pain that I still feel; and help me share it… but they cannot.

The Resignation

Chapter 23

We are all tormented at death with the remembrance of our sins, and seeing that we have done no penance, it tempts us to despair. It tells us that there is a perfect remedy; namely, to accept death and unite our death with resignation. I do not doubt that he who is guilty of offending God, and accepts death willingly in satisfaction for his sins, will immediately obtain a pardon. Anger, when carried internally by ourselves for long periods of time, is often transformed into feelings of guilt. We reproach ourselves for not having done enough, not seeing or understanding, or being there for them. We would have liked to have been more present, or to be at their side during the last moments—but we just cannot resign from all this.

You may have often heard: "We are more of what we have lost once we have lost it." In the context of grieving, the feeling of emptiness in life created by the absence of our deceased, reveals the importance of the bond shared with them. This acknowledgement causes us, the survivors, to be particularly hard on ourselves; to develop remorse and guilt, since we are here and they are not.

Put another way, faced with a lack of meaning over the death of our loved one, we are tempted to redirect our anguish internally; towards ourselves. We just cannot resign from it. This natural propensity shoulders us with a great source of suffering, contributing to a sense of guilt. I would argue, guilt is more present in the context of mourning after a drama like mine (i.e. violent death of my child). In this case, parents tend to take a more direct role in the responsibility of what happened, and this translates into a mindset along the lines of: "If only I had known" or "I wish I could have been there for them."

Feeling guilty comes in many ways, especially in the case of an unresolved murder. This feeling of guilt is then even harder to share, for fear of being misunderstood by those around you. And of course, our guilt is sometimes one of the last voices that connects us to the deceased; to let go of our guilt gives the impression of wanting to definitively cut the bond of attachment.

Guilt is a pernicious form that manifests from our internally directed anger; we *must* be very cognizant of this. Avoiding things that we did not or cannot control is crucial for overcoming your guilt. In the long run, this allows us to forgive others without breaking the bond that binds us to the deceased, and often marks the beginning of a new relationship with him. A more peaceful relationship. It is called *resignation*. Eventually, we resign from anger and guilt.

Living with volatile emotions during mourning can be daunting. The fear of losing control is paralyzing, yet it is good because pent up emotions need to be released. I assure you, your mind and soul will feel better once you have released some of that pressure that adds weight to your suffering. Giving free rein to your emotions (sadness, despair, hopelessness) for a short period of time, will help you displace yourself from the inundated perception of being overwhelmed. This in turn will assist you in preventing your anger from overtaking every aspect of your life.

Most people understand our suffering and guilt; they understand that we have the right to be angry at the injustice we are going through. The important thing is to find a way that suits you to live with these emotions: writing, sports, exchanges, walking… To further this, you may try using the internet. I suppose this is in direct opposition to what I described earlier in this book. But the internet does have one upside; to network with others like yourself, others who have lost a child. For example, you can discover the testimonies of others in mourning, and share your grief experience with them through blogs, chat groups and online group therapy sessions.

It is important to find the place and the appropriate person who will welcome your emotions without judgment about what happened. From his death, I keep the image of an amazing young man: original, resourceful and impressive. I still see him tapping his controllers of his old Panasonic television, his melancholy face watching me go out early after dinner to earn a living because my regular income and tiny child support was not enough to feed six kids. I feel the bombardment of emotions he was in when we divorced. Even today, I am unable to measure the consequences of all these actions on the lives of my children, who were entering adolescence at that time.

Today the song *Tues-Moi* (Kill-Me) that was played in church at Michael's funeral weighs on my soul with extreme heaviness and sorrow. It has accompanied me for many years now, both as a reminder the injustice around his death, and my dark times. My most painful memory, is undoubtedly the discovery of his body, but one day I would like to allow the right to say the terrible phrase in the most popular journals. I cannot stand it anymore, the success and the silence of my son's murderers. It kills me. Even if all the priests in the churches would pray for my wish, I don't think they would understand that his mother will never be able to publish and even write the great novel she has always dreamed of, the work of her life. "They cut off his wings, took away all the light and kept it for themselves alone, they are condemned by others to shut up, to stay in the shadows." Why are they not gnawed by an abyssal guilt? And to continue all this time in something indecent.

How can I try to understand that my son, who did not even have the chance to live to his twenty-third birthday, end up on such a path? Once again, I am directly confronted with the haunting question: "Why?"

One day, if justice is served, will it be enough to buy them, the murderers, a house in Hell? And, allow me to retreat from my nightmare? God the Father has refused my request many times, on the pretext of not wanting to fight. I probably did not know how to propose my prayers to him. Simply, me the missed mother, daring to appear in front of him to give alms for the assassins of Michael. A boy who could never afford a car, ever so modest and giving, despite a lifetime of poverty.

I started my resignation one year after he was passed away. I think we all go through a phase where we miss the notion of a perfect life? Or the idea of how life should be? As part of my recovery, and in an effort to begin communicating again with those closest to me; I moved to Calgary to be with all my family. My daughter was here with her family and so was Robert Jr. I wanted to enjoy more time with my kids and my grandchildren.

We do not know how to be grateful and appreciative towards life until we encounter death. Unfortunately, it is not as easy for everyone, as we all go through different hardships. Even through the hardships, we should always be aware that there are others out there: like us or worse off than us. Every year, when I travel to undeveloped countries, I am humbled, and reminded of my good fortune. For instance, eating nutritious food, taking a hot shower or having clean drinking water.

The Unfair Decision

Chapter 24

Sitting at my computer, I try to forget that it has been seven years since his death. Yes, seven squandered years during which investigators tried, and now; have let us down due to the absurdity of our legal system. I find that I am left with my residual grief, and without an explanation why they murdered him… without leaving him the time to say goodbye. I simply ask for fairness or justice to be found. But no, the system tells us that they did enough investigating and that his case is now transferred to File 13. To be dungeoned, like so many other murdered children.

Why are so many people disappointed so easily with decisions that are made in court and in our system. Sometimes people cannot believe their ears as a ruling is reached by a judge or a jury.

I am not condoning the police per se, but the system in which they work is at fault. The investigators are overloaded with cases, forty to fifty a year each, so that they cannot possibly dedicate enough time to each murder. In this way, things are overlooked, missed and unresolved. There is something wrong with our system that lets guilty criminals walk free, because evidence cannot be processed to determine and expose their crimes.

It is incomprehensible that those officer's function without the necessary resources and manpower to track, capture and prosecute murderers of innocent people like Michael. Eventually these investigators, through no fault of their own, simply have to dismiss each case, placing it in File 13, or declaring it a *Cold Case*. Never to be opened again, without new evidence.

What I thought, or what everybody thought, was an adventure for him turned into a nightmare. Michael did not do anything to make this happen; he was just in the wrong place at the wrong time. And sadly, we cannot do anything about it. I have reasoned that the killer's silence is to conceal their identities. This silence disturbs me more every day. Hopefully, one day I will meet them. I have always been looking for them. And on that day, trying not to be afraid or angry, I will open my heart to that crime and let happiness enter.

I still believe in God, but frankly, I do not believe in justice! And, I don't believe in the romantic image of an old judge with a long black tunic. In my opinion, our legal system has become distorted by circumstance and obscure interpretations of the law. These days, the criminals have more chances to prove their innocence, than us, the parents or victims, have to prove their guilt.

We look at the sky and hope that our angel will do something powerful and bring the evidence needed to put those criminals behind bars before the face of the judge. But we can't, because there is no way to have decent proof with the absurdity of the law and the notion of *reasonable doubt*. I'm not attacking the exasperating system, but if I could do justice myself, and if they were captured; I would have granted them an appropriate punishment: the same as what they did to my son.

But this would not be fair to my other children. That's why I claim unfairness, injustice or the absence of God. I know that there are lots of people out there who brought up the improbability of finding my son's killers. In the past seven years, investigators have aimed all the evidences of people's testimonies and interrogated all the suspects they had. Today, the most popular rumour in St-Georges de Beauce is that Michael had been tied, hanged in a shed, beaten, stabbed, had his arms and legs broken, then put in an insulation bag because he was bleeding too much and transported to Notre-Dame-des-Pins near the railway. This was heard by an amazingly large number of people. It is with a very strong probability, and there are many unanswerable questions, but it is precisely because of so many of those stories that the investigators decided seven years afterward to file his murder as a cold case. Just like in a box, the same I did with the black bag. For seven years they tried everything, turned all clues over and looked at them from every angle and often came close to proving and finalizing, but it seems like the killers do not exist, or that no proof can be held against them. In twenty-five years of practice, the officers said they had never seen any murder case so complicated, with so many different stories and so many suspects. Of all these suspects, a Lafreniere, a certain Drouin, or a Miss Blanchette were the most common. It seems to me that these suspects in the St-Georges area were trying to gain notoriety, gain a patch on a vest or appear as though they were trying to become famous for the murder of my son.

Unfortunately, they; the murderers, do not think straight and think we; the citizens, are stupid. Humans should not warm to such crudeness. Rivers of speculations about the Hell's Angels and my brothers snitch, not to mention all the tears of blood that have been squandered over the mystery of the murder of my son. That fact has been suppressed and deviated from the truth. Hell's Angels don't kill the children of an ex-member, and especially not a nephew. The police have denied several times that my son's murder has a relation to them. You are probably asking yourself if it is a coincidence that my brother turned in his vest at the same time that Michael disappeared. The answer is yes. He was talking about this for months and was obsessed that they would kill him.

One thing is for certain: if the provincial police have been in control of my son's case, it would have been taken seriously right from the beginning. This in comparison to how his case was misappropriated by the incompetence of the municipal police of St-Georges. To this day, I believe the killers would be in jail as there was enough evidence in the apartment to find them. Very little was known about what happened when Michael disappeared and when we advised the police, his case was taken lightly. There was no reasonable way to make officer Lacroix believe that Michael was in danger or possibly dead. I have a grudge against this unscrupulous and egotistical policeman.

In the middle of the week, when we went to the apartment with him, he was convinced that Michael had gone somewhere on a road trip to grow some weed. It was clear to us that he was in danger and that the matter for us was way more serious. In a police unit, there are three levels: light, medium and high cases. I knew that Michael was gone and there was no way to logically reason with that police officer. He was convinced that I or my brother Johnny were depressed or were fabricating things. Thus, in the words of faith, I was imploring him to believe that my son was dead, and that there was not a place he could be growing weed. I was so hurt. A better course would have been to abandon the idea and let him believe in his stupid story, allowing himself an easy ride to destroy the case of my son. He never allowed my brother and me to rigorously vet our story. Decimated by his stubborn and snobbish thoughts, he allowed the landlord to empty the apartment that contained all the evidence, persuaded that my son had just left without paying his due. Discrimination and ignorance are altogether grounds for selfish, incompetent and inefficient people.

Not surprisingly today, the officer of the Sûreté du Quebec says that Michael's case had been handled poorly, and that the municipal police were useless and destroyed all the evidence to find those criminals.

I hoped that the municipal police could recognize their mistakes and that the progression of my son's case would have been very different to this day. But instead, the evidence that has been destroyed is still in my head in so many versions, the most unpleasant feeling for a crying mom.

The character of all those books and movies is still in my head. I hope that they are proud of themselves and make themselves desensitized to the horror movie that I live in. I am pleased to tell you how petty, unjust and unforgiving I am about those control freaks.

Unfortunately, creative intelligence and competency arrived to let in this matter today and therefore they cannot hold anybody responsible for vindictive, capricious and unjust people, which is ridiculous, even if my son's murder had nothing to do with the Hell's Angels. My brother was just declared a snitch, so the case should have been transferred immediately to the Sûreté du Quebec to the department of Crimes Against the Persons.

I'm not sure that the municipal police ever wrote down all my stories, but I will always attribute that to the society they like to deal with, which is the dealer's scrapyard, even if it seems that it is presumably an authentic friend or close colleague of the industry. Michael has been sadly used, and even if I know today that the chase to find them is no greater that finding how a hurricane sweeps down a city and nobody can predict how many houses will be destroyed, the evidence of finding them are the same.

Originating from St. Georges to Notre-Dame-des-Pins, I will probably never know were all this began. From the crazy drug-addicted mother Kathy who pretends to know them and how they killed him, and hearing that he was bleeding so much so he had to be wrapped in an insulation bag and transported in the trunk of a car like a mutt, to be thrown like a piece of junk in a scrapyard.

Will I one day have the luck of assembling all the pieces together and finalizing the puzzle? The odds against fully assembling a good case are the same as shuffling fifty-four cards and cutting the ace of hearts on the first try. They say you have fifty-four chances, but I don't think so, as every time you have to shuffle the same fifty-four cards, which multiplies the chances by fifty-four, but if we could eliminate a card every time, it would make our chances a bit higher.

This, in a nutshell, is the creation of gossip that originates from a little city like St. Georges. This argument can only be made by people who don't understand a criminal case, by somebody who thinks that they can go ahead and create a story to make themselves interesting. I'm not sure if those people read the law and know that you can't report the words of another person, but that it takes facts, and those facts need to be proven in the head of a judge without a reasonable doubt.

The people who misappropriated the murder from improbable facts always take the same general form and it doesn't make any difference to the proof of evidence. The masquerade was always the same. The guys and gals go into a bar and show off how they contributed to Michael's murder. A sexy girl around thirty years old in a lascivious fancy dress, displaying tattoo designs on her perfectly sculpted body, one near her voluptuous breast, a rose inked on her neck and a couple more on the arms. She is meeting with us and pretending that she was used by the Hell's Angels; she says she was beaten to make her shut up but she came to us and tried to convince us that Michael was framed. She pretends that she carried him in the trunk of her car. Stipulating that he was beaten and stabbed to death. That was the first story we heard, the night we were coming back from the cemetery where we buried him. That's the day my nightmares got worse. It was a descendance into Hell. Later on, in the week, the same phenomenon would take place in another bar, and she would tell the same story. Police would search for months to find the car. One day, they traced a car corresponding to this story, with some blood from once upon a time transporting my son's dying body. FBI called to come to Calgary and collect my blood. That's what they need to prove that the DNA matched mine.

Often adorned with all the virtues, DNA is not the queen of proofs; error of manipulation, analysis or conservation can ruin the test. My boss was certainly not impressed by seeing an FBI agent in his office and it was the ultimate knockdown for my career.

Even if a DNA sample would have made it possible to clarify the judicial case of my son, in addition to being used as evidence to establish the guilt of one of the suspects or even the innocence of some people who were accused unfairly, I wish that this time the forensic lab would have extracted and analyzed his genetic code.

In that scene, they thought they had found the car, and the blood in the trunk was Michael's. How much chance is there to find a car with blood in the trunk? On the face of that massive vision of the report that came and crushed down my only hope, not just feeling it but hoping to finally realize that there will be no testimony and no sufficient evidence to establish a miracle in that falsehood once again. They have the identity of the deceased, but because of the complexity of the law I have to prove that Michael was my son. But all the procedures needed have to be correctly extolled as they can't be used for evidence to arrest those assassins that are still free like hummingbirds flying in the blue sky of St-Georges de Beauce.

Have people ever realized how much that costs society and how painful and torturous it can be for us parents? Imagine you are there at your job and an FBI agent comes in and says: "I need to speak to Madame X." Of course, you work in a small office and nobody has ever heard your story. You try to keep a solid face. This all arises in your brain like data and you have to become the compatible mom with two alternatives to choose from: positive or negative. While those officers bring you into the small kitchen of an uninsulated office, where everybody can hear your conversation and gossip about the way he died and what they think they heard. The simulation to your brain has become like software and you become quite adept at flipping this story to something else. Why does that have to happen? Why do we have to feel so miserable as parents of a murdered child? Why doesn't all gossip aim in the correct direction? Why can't people just demonstrate sympathy? We, for most of us, have all been religiously brought up the same way. I go to the same Catholic church, which teaches us how to love. This is the first and greatest command we learn, that we should love our neighbors as ourselves and that we should never take revenge and not hold grudges against the children of our fellow human beings, that we will honour our father and mother and that we should follow the law and fulfill it in one word: trepidation. I can't fill my heart with these words anymore, many times I see the face of the devil overlapping the face of God.

Even if I have been impressionable and brought up with the most religious beliefs, I am mixed up and try to go in the right direction. People who haven't previously experienced this can't understand and it saps the illusion of a kid with amazement. Even strangers seem to wear the masks of hypocrites. Sometimes you think that surprisingly there will be someone who understands, but it turns to water.

I say all this to demonstrate how much pain and sorrow we have. The formidable mixture that is in my brain has been powered for seven years with simulation and false interpretation and has released all those unsupportable endorphins.

Once, as a child, I heard my mom pray to the Virgin Mary for my dad not to kill us. My mom's voice was murmuring the recitation of her prayer. I could almost but not quite hear the words, which seemed to have a serious impact on her demand. From the moment I could talk, I had to make out the words to thank God or the Virgin Mary. Many times, I was taken back to hearing the voice of my mom imploring them to save us. Was that enough to impress the unintelligible speech intoned in my voice today?

Even if somebody would hurt me and promise me that I'd go to heaven, I would still wait for that miracle to come.

Strange, because right now I just believe that each of us come into this world and somebody makes us think that we are going to leave happy and raise a beautiful family with no obstacles. Until the day, without knowing why, we deviate from that purpose. From the standpoint of daily life, we all know that we should help our neighbour's friends or family. Above all this, we all know that we can't always decide the course of life and that sometimes the path or the direction it takes is completely different from what we expected. We think that in approximately two years we will get married, but our loved one can get killed in a car accident and if he doesn't, we imagine that after that wedding, in two other years, we will start building a family.

Above all, for those whose family are their wellbeing, we put all our happiness through our children, who we think will be there for us in our old days. We find it hard to imagine how, without them, life can be good; would we even want to live without them?

Shall we discuss such questions, as we all know that our children will die after us?

I brought you to the conclusion that people, through paroxysms of hatred, hypocrisy and corrupt influences could commit the irreproachable. There are murderers who will act like murderers but there are some who will act more like sophisticated humans and you will have no idea that they could have done such an irreparable act. A great deal of deviation of common sense, which, in a moment of aberration, will flee.

There is no real link to a morality when there is no connection with the evolution of the crime itself. It ranges from the naivety that evolved one day in my son's head to be underlying motivations of those individuals. I received a lot of messages from people stating that they are with me and understand my pain but I'm not sure they do understand that I need that consolation. My own thoughts, my feelings and everything I love in life was recalculated. And please stop telling me that you know who killed my son or know something about the murder, then you never call or never show up at the stupid meeting that I took time to book. Please shut up, it's better. Better for my soul who is living in hope that one day that hero will finally talk.

I have achieved a lot, but I still have so much to finish. The total futility of my son's investigation has built in me an omnipotent power that no lord could stop. I will not go quietly without finding those guilty assholes. If in the future that requires violence, I hope they will remember how or who brought it on.

My rifle is loaded, even if I don't have one, and I am ready for the war that they have started. Even if I'm a pacifist, I can deliver it the same way they inflicted it. The best part for me would be to see them suffer one hundred times more that Michael did. Will I have that chance, as justice is not in store for them? They get the comfort of a bed, three meals a day, and the discretion to vent themselves to other criminals like them. I find this puzzling that criminals have so many more benefits than us, the parents of the victims, who are left with basically no help. We have to continue to work amidst the turmoil of our emotions. We have to pay our own psychedelic sessions to not break the law ourselves or commit an irreparable mistake; those people have no clue as to what we go through. We are the slaves of the justice which serves criminals ways better than us, the crying moms.

I hope that one day there will be a law with no mercy, and that for our sake the truth will be revealed before the knife connects with the punishment of its blade, that they will suffer for eternity for their sins that we are completely ignorant of and that the wrath of God will show no mercy.

Friends have suggested to me many times that I hire a bad guy to do justice myself. But unfortunately, I have no name to go after. I just want a feeling of expectation and the desire to punish them for the vicious act they did, and peace of mind while I live.

I wonder how happy I would be and how my personal life would be. It's not like if I'm not happy, but some days I have to try hard to prove my happiness and find meaning to this story.

This feeling that I'm not alone is true. It's typical of many people like me who believe they are inherently sick and that teaching our kids that we evolved by a blind chance and being that negative shouldn't be on our daily menu. But when the evil follows, you have to restrain yourself from the ultimate fact that this does not only happen to others.

Even if we still think about morality and that we should embrace every beautiful moment in life, we should all have the right to this closure. It is hard to believe that human nature has been ill, as we all possess the same feeling. Wrenching compassion isn't feeling that we shouldn't have to beg.

We all have the urge toward empathy when we see an orphan, an animal with three legs or an old widow suffering from loneliness. I wish that people would have this for us, the parents whose children die of a criminal act. Isn't goodness incompatible with the theory of crime? How do we know the point they are involved? How do we know if they are in danger if they don't ask or we didn't see the signs? Where are the good Samaritans for us when we need a shoulder to cry on? Is it necessary for journalists to spread all that bad news? That precisely is the conduct of a selfish society in the form of information that people hear without putting it in context. Because they don't make an analysis of themselves and compete for the best communication (which needs to be trash or ruthless stories) to gain attention. The parents that survive in this world will be the ones who will succeed in surviving at the expense of the gossips and rivals. It's like the whole idea is to make us feel bad and to destroy us completely. With the stress of our loss, that is precisely what the hearsay does.

Of course, things have changed, and people today know the truth, but my whole point is that people are way too gullible to the gossips on social media and the news and instead should go directly to the right information. Even if they apologize, they cannot get away with the pain they have caused me, even if they did publish the opposite the day after. There was a clear distinction between their act and what was needed.

Do those people who hold up the newspaper as an inspiration to destroy a family have the slightest notion of what it is really like to lose a child? Not only do we hope that the death penalty would come back for the murderers, but somewhere in our hearts we wish, because of their comments, that they would go through the same loss. Cursing families who are already hurt is the unfortunate best to be undergone. What shocks me is that every time there are people hurt by a horrible story, they don't even know what really happened. They probably will never know. People today should base their lives on the beautiful thing the victims have done and stop speculating for the families.

I wish I could have the political power of the prime minister and make lapidating legal again. I don't believe there is law in the world that cannot bulldoze the assassins. This is an insult to we grieving parents who have spent all those years without closure. Without this we cannot live. We should have enough investigators to continue to search for as long as is needed. No, our justice system puts them at ease to prove their innocence.

Men can never do justice themselves, as it is preserved by the law. My main purpose has not been to show that we shouldn't get our justice from the police, but it's to show that we really need a bigger budget and be like the other places who have the criminals in jail and it is up to them to prove they are not guilty, not the opposite.

I have demonstrated many times that we should be heard on the facts, that we don't get the chance to share the cases of our deceased, although we should have the right to access the file, as we know the most about them.

If we did, we would strictly observe the facts and think about it justly and properly so that we could cross-examine anybody who we think are guilty, and we could stone them to death.

Isn't the law able to undo the damage and make it all right? Is it right that if the criminals are unsatisfied with this prison cell or his judgement, they have the right to ask for another cell or trial? Is it right that we are not allowed to execute disobedient killers anymore? Is it right that when we are not able to prove that he was not 5'11" instead of 6', they release suspects because there is doubt in the heads of the judges? Well, there is no denying that, from a justice point of view, there is a huge improvement that needs to be made over the cruel ogre of the provincial justice. Indeed, the law, if it exists, is surely the one of the greatest stupid innovations of the century.

If the criminal turns to be wise and anticipates being not guilty, he has the right to have a review. The superior court then has to hear him and later delights to be presented with a different eye. Then the lawyers bear out their crime and they make them go to a mental hospital which will rehabilitate them and throw them back in society in less than five years. Bravo, bravo, bravo...

Although most victims feel they have the opportunity to obtain emotional closure, many victims remain angry but with less intensity. They learned about day-to-day operations and discussed the importance of the grieving process and how decent memorials can help people with emotional closure.

In turn, victims would be better placed to find emotional closure and be able to move on from the offence that they have been carrying around in their emotional baggage, and seek closure by writing a forgiveness letter to themselves.

Therefore, we passed from symbolic actions with great cultural and emotional impact to a collaborative process that was seen as a pathway to a new beginning, enabling a practical and legal closure as well as an emotional and perhaps moral one.

Speech enables each participant to bring a personal closure to every emotional session and to make their contributions to ending in a good way.

Sometimes it involves strong emotional debate, but ultimately it is a debate of words settled by a dramatic vote. I would agree with my honorable AFPAD friends that it has become a very emotional issue.

Things should be put into service so that the total workforce of the privatized companies will increase slightly after the closure of the blast furnace, as with the murdered.

It is our sincere hope that this action may bring a measure of closure to those who still grieve for their loved ones. Any other decision would result in the closure and loss of numerous lives. If the issue is settled, the case is closed; the ways for closure will not be discussed again. We need to be clear about the fact that people are indulging in emotional manipulation here.

It was a remarkable day, one of those days which makes you even more enthusiastic about that amazing victory of human history which is finding the killers.

The framework negotiated with them is clear and it involves firm and unambiguous respect for the victims regarding closure on agreed sentences. When judges and juries have not given a tangible response to the victims, when judges impose the benefits of reasonable doubt on us, it justifies the blockade on killer's grounds, stating that in the absence of personnel loyal to the people on the planet side of the crossings, it could not permit the opening of the criminal's trials, even with the coordination for government activities in any territory or non-governmental organization. His last breath was on 15 September 2011. We are still looking for those killers after seven years, at the time of the writing of this book.

In family values, ethics teach our children to forgive sins, but how deep is the sin or the crime if the compassion is with the real crime? It's admirable that the good people have to endure and support that stupid law. I refer especially to the law in Quebec which relies on a bunch of crap and nonsense. It is almost as rare to obtain good judgement as to find a new virgin bride.

But symbolically, didn't Adam and Eve commit sin without being married? What kind of ethical justice is it that condemns every victim before the trial starts? To inherit the sin that was rightly committed, we need the authority to find those responsible in one way. But which way is the right way?

But now the sadomasochist has incarnated himself into an ill man, the schizophrenic who can torture a family of three and kill them and be released with good medication, and through the worship as the redeemer of all our sins, we can all be crazy for five years.

AFPAD says that judges and juries have not given a "tangible response" to the victims. Therefore, if the project closure document for phase 1 of AFPAD is not submitted to the governing judges, there is no smart closure, not like an automatic power closure or a system with movement and detection.

In addition to that, we have introduced a new closing system which we call "Snap-In Closure," which leads to savings for the government. And above the flow, we have to live in the area of a pharmaceutical production plant that produces sleeping pills for depression where we are getting the Getting Closure Processing System for a couple hours. They completely fail to grasp the real nature of the conflict. There are no questions. We are victims, that's it. The creators of the laws know just the symptoms of our illness and what they see as the great enemy is the money, but we cannot exist without appropriate treatments.

In the Common Closure, the package is assembled tighter. The reason why there is no memorial today is because there is no "closure for many." The physical body is not found. Science has a form of tools to identify them but there is nothing to test with.

Even if several recommendations have been addressed to the magistrates through improvements, there is no magic system in place where we can bargain mental health, correct medication and fairness. Only time can tell, but there is no indication of how much time it will take to find the body or the murderers. We are jeopardized, tauntingly telling people that we hope that the police will teach people how to find DNA or violate the system and do justice ourselves.

So to all of those intelligent citizens in Canada and in Quebec who have been listening to us, to all our extraterrestrial colleagues who have actively participated in the work of this committee, I would like to remind you that the work of this committee is drawing to a close, and that maybe in a couple of months as a result of another closure, which means that we will have to conclude his death in less than five hours and live for the rest of our lives with the mediocrity of the direct evidence that strikes against us. Our government invested in expensive telescopes for the criminals to admit their sin or prepare forgiveness, nothing for the sole purpose of searching or orbiting us to stability or more help for our investigators. Once again, he missed the satellite system. It's just like searching for signals in the sky to find aliens where a number of systems in the sky are illuminated. I praise our judges who impose the benefits of reasonable doubts on us, it justifies with mediocrity and blocks the killers to be guilty, stating that in the absence of evidence, civilization that is loyal to the people on this planet is astride the crossings, it permits the opening of the criminal's trails and makes them powerful enough to see all the planets that is on earth. In one word, they are allowed to see all the stars in the sky while we see the clouds. There was nothing particular on the night of 15 September to September 2011, but in the universe, someone was taking his last breath. And this was my son. Who would think about that matter, but in fact we live in an extremely mediocre place where the system propels the killers free for almost seven years?

I often talk to Michael in my thoughts. I hope he is in paradise and for a moment I could be with him, just a moment to tell him how dearly I love him, and I could take care of his hurt in his endless sleep. I remember the day he left, the last words he told me were: "Take care of yourself and the kids." Even if I pray, I cry and I shout his name for him to come home without any explanation. Whether your child is honest or a bandit, your mother is still your mother, I will always have the right to tell him softly and tenderly in his ear that I love him, until my last sleep.

I'm lucky to have my mom and I often tell her how much I love her. Nobody in the world will take her place in my life. A mother is the most beautiful person to us, giving us the moments of our life. I am proud to be with her and that she is there for me.

When I am at the bar next, I'll take a drink for Michael, who in the eyes of the law is the forgotten one. I am forced to put behind me that he would probably be sitting here with me if things had been different. He was a great kid, and I miss him dearly. I thought we would always be together for life or at least that he would be the one to bury me in the ground. Bury me in the soil that is going to be cold soon, where winter will leave her white coat and where now, I will be making snow-angels with my grandchildren, thinking that they are images of him.

Conclusion

Even if all the possible evidence is collected at the scene of a possible crime and must be transported to facilities where it can be described, labelled and photographed, with a serial number, under the most secure and confidential conditions, what does it matter? Even if all human remains are sent to medical facilities, to the morgue, and undergo an autopsy (Greek term meaning "to see with one's own eyes"), what does it matter? I experienced this atmosphere for too many years. The silence of his assassins is the thing that still haunts me; not as much as it used to, but I still resigned myself to the idea, and it was at that point that I knew I had done my sorrow, where my son had passed away and it was time for me to carry on.

If love is only for a moment, then so is life. We, parents of deceased children, would love to spend a last moment with them. We all say, "If life is only a memory, I want my memory to be from you." Our hearts are so fragile, just like the scent of spring in the breeze.

Let's get on with what an unknown tomorrow brings, to be together and think about what infinity holds for us. We all have a heartfelt melody, a little birdie with all his wonderful colours, that reminds us of our sweet child, our darling, a part of our soul.

I braced myself for too long to face the tragedy that ripped my heart apart. It is ripped like a piece of white satin paper because death takes its toll on our hearts so immensely.

If we manage to see properly, our vision is too short, our methods without depth, and if we do not consider things open-minded and relaxed, we turn our sorrow into a major difficulty and what was initially only insignificant became significant. In other words: We create a lot of our own suffering.

If only I could discern in my suffering a single atom of utility, or fairness. I suppose I would tolerate it better. My disarray was not only due to this external thing, but it depended a lot on the perception of others. I contemplate the day I have the power to change that perception.

Suffering passes, but to have suffered does not pass. Even if you chastise your mind, lead it to happiness, the undisciplined world leads you to more suffering.

I think to live through mourning is not what they would have liked it to be. Some lucky ones have closure; for us, the door hasn't closed and is left forthcoming, even if the pain finds a comfy place in our wrecked hearts. In some ways, we know that one little thing can make it burst, with the same vigor and hatred as before.

My life has changed drastically, and the facts stopped me from ascending into a big black hole. I wrote this manuscript practically for all of us who are looking for light at the end of the tunnel. Many times, I thought I would no longer have a family life. I did not want to replace the one I had, or all my children, but in return, my current partner has a daughter born on the same day as Michael. Even if his vivacity can't bloom, I'm not unhappy with my current existence. The path was long, very long, but it's worth the effort to believe in love again and imagine a happy family. We have now a beautiful rebuilt family of nine.

I had to let go of my misfortunes and continue in the unknown of love. Without a safety net, alone with my two youngest children, I kept praying, keeping hope, thriving and remaining confident that I could face death and move forward. It took me a long time to overcome this tragedy because I could not forget about Michael, and the injustice of his murderers. Today I have discovered happiness, mourning deserves deep sadness, merits that linger, but instead I was twirled left and right to forget. We must continue to talk about them, even after all these years. We must honour their death and hope for our future.

Today, I see Michael without any pain in me, the line of pain, of toil, is silent. He approaches slowly and then disintegrates with his bruised body. Even If some days I cherish the image of the golden death, it's because I am calendared by my dark thoughts. This diabolical image sometimes appears in me and accompanies me on the new path that I pursue—in the beginning for you, and now for me.

Even if the years ahead are still heavy in my heart, I saw myself too many times being pushed down a desolate path by this trajectory in my life. Have we become slaves to the vast majority of our frustrations, our sufferings, our sadness? So, the important thing is not what we support, but how to support it. When we suffer, there is nothing more frustrating that nobody understands our suffering. But by suffering we come to better understand the suffering of others.

Many humans think that seeking happiness means remaining indifferent to the suffering of others, which is a tragic mistake. Suffering has forced my creativity; it does not mean that one has to be forced to suffer to become creative, but if there is a meaning to life there must be a sense of suffering. Suffering makes us selfish because it absorbs us whole. It is later that the souvenir of the suffering we went through teaches us compassion. Suffering comes as much from understanding as it does from ignorance.

Suffering allows certain qualities to surface, such as perseverance, resilience, and altruism. Without these qualities, we would perhaps never have had the opportunity to manifest themselves as much.

One day you will see this ordeal as wealth. There is no metamorphosis without pain. I had the power to find serenity in the suffering, which was for me the proof of a great will and a great knowledge. If you think that life has let you down again and you see that all your world is crumbling around you, do not forget that the sun always comes after the rain. Open your heart wide, do not look elsewhere, listen to him, he will tell you.

Do not miss the chance to be loved or to love. The heart becomes lighter when we are in love. If someday you think that nothing in your life is good and that like a bohemian you are wandering in the night soothing your sorrow, remember, there is always someone waiting for you in the sky.

But life sometimes makes us a slave to our memories. Between us, what does the past matter? There is the future, that's why you have to put the love in your heart.

Because one day the impossible, the unimaginable happens, and becomes the reality. A child goes away, somewhere else, beyond this existence. After the shock, after the chaos, there remains a slim hope that gives life back to us, the desire to continue—their soul remains alive, love wins, love is stronger than death. But the way to get there is long, very long, so long.

Shattered by the death of Michael, who was swept away by a blistering murder at the age of twenty-two, one evening, by chance, I sent a message to a stranger, like a bottle in the sea. I was shocked when, against all odds, an answer immediately came: "We must accept to live under his protection. He is not the one who needs you, it is you who needs him. Love cannot end. The living who have left can leave us signs." For more than a year, the close and almost daily dialogue continues between me and this deeply hurt mother. May it also be a sign for all those who look for hope?

I got swept up in a story to the point of feeling euphoric, only to see my dreams come tumbling down a few weeks or months later when the evidence went sour. You're in a positive state of mind but you are haunted by thoughts about maybe finding the killers, and what might have been if they find them. Sometimes I lust after the early days where I thought he was still here and I had stopped mourning his loss. And dreaming about losing this tension that it created between me and the people around me, hoping that these experiences would have nothing at all to do with killers and it would be suicide. This message was unbelievable, you'd be surprised to learn the real reason you keep feeling let down in the love department, and why understanding this is the key to finally feeling like you've found it.

"Today, the best way to soften my torment is to relive the suffering of my retreat from my nightmare. God the Father has refused many times my request on the pretext of not wanting to fight with Satan." I probably had no idea how to propose it to him. Sincerely, I am confused; me, the missed mother, daring to appear in front of the Almighty Father to give Him the alms of the assassins of my dear son. Despite the lifetime of an honest citizen. Michael Carreau, son of Marya Fredette, was found savagely murdered on 5 November 2011, by two hunters near an abandoned railway

Nine weeks after the terrible night of the 15 to 16 September 2011. Michael was last seen alive at the Bar le Vieux St-Georges around 3 A.M. He entered a car and was never seen alive again. Seven years have passed and nobody has confessed. The silence of those assassins still kills me.

About the Author

Born in Montreal and raised in La Beauce, Quebec, Marya Fredette raised six lovely children by herself. After graduating from college and a bitter divorce, she obtained three degrees in mechanical and design engineering technology, structural building engineering technology, and insurance brokerage for the home, automotive and commercial industry. Without any support from her ex-husband, Marya was employed during the day and worked in bars at night in order to make ends meet. Within a year of working as a bartender she became a successful bar owner and managed to own six bars in a two-year period in the St. George's de Beauce area.

A Mothers Tears is Marya's first book, detailing the heartless murder of her son, Michael, her fourth child. Now relocated to Calgary, Alberta, Marya enjoys her rebuilt family of nine with a partner who has a successful career in orthodontics. Marya's hopes and aspirations are the same as every woman's, but she dreams of being an example that a positive life outcome is possible after a malevolent divorce and the death of a child. Marya asserts nothing but strength and has always believed that happiness is attainable if you profoundly have faith in positive thoughts and visualize your success. She says: Always hold onto your values and expect nothing but the best from yourself.